Behold! ה

The Beauty of Woman

Written by: Tracy L. Edwards

© 2021 by Tracy L. Edwards

Publisher information

All rights reserved. No part of this publication may be reproduced, stored in a retrieval system, or transmitted in any form or by any means—for example, electronic, photocopy, recording—without the prior written permission of Tracy L. Edwards. The only exception is brief quotations in printed reviews.

Library of Congress Cataloging-in-Publication Data

Edwards, Tracy L., 1966–
    Behold! /*The Beauty of Woman.*

ISBN 978-1-7355944-3-9

All scripture quotations, unless otherwise indicated, are taken from the New King James Version®. Copyright © 1982 by Thomas Nelson, Inc. Used by permission. All rights reserved.

Scripture quotations from The Authorized (King James) Version. Rights in the Authorized Version in the United Kingdom are vested in the Crown. Reproduced by permission of the Crown's patentee, Cambridge University Press. Scriptures quoted from the King James Version are represented by (KJV)

Scripture quotations marked (NIV) are taken from the Holy Bible, New International Version®, NIV®. Copyright © 1973, 1978, 1984 by Biblica, Inc.™ Used by permission of Zondervan. All rights reserved worldwide. www.zondervan.com

Scripture quotations marked MSG are taken from THE MESSAGE, copyright © 1993, 2002, 2018 by Eugene H. Peterson. Used by permission of NavPress, represented by Tyndale House Publishers. All rights reserved.

Scripture quotations taken from the Amplified® Bible (AMP), Copyright © 2015 by The Lockman Foundation. Used by permission. www.Lockman.org

Scripture quotations marked (CEV) are from the Contemporary English Version Copyright © 1991, 1992, 1995 by American Bible Society, Used by Permission.

Dedication

To the One who created me in His image.

To my husband, Steve: I love you.

To my children and grandchildren: wear His image well.

To Freedom Church: shine brightly in His glory.

Contents

Introduction — p.1

Instructions — p.4

    Chapter 1—The Beginning — p.7
    Chapter 2—By God's Design — p.14
    Chapter 3—Bliss — p.26
    Chapter 4—A Comparable Help Meet — p.38
    Chapter 5—In The Presence Of — p.51
    Chapter 6—Well, That Explains It! — p.69
    Chapter 7—You Cannot Undo What You Have Done — p.89
    Chapter 8—Redemption —p. 119
    Chapter 9—The Freedom of Submission — p.136
    Chapter 10—Behold! A Virtuous Woman — p.174
    Chapter 11—An Overcoming Lifestyle — p.196
    Chapter 12—A Heart's Hope — p.229

Resources — p.241

Acknowledgments — p.244

About the Author — p.245

Introduction

I knew who I wanted to be and what I wanted to do when I was young. I wanted to be a wife who had dinner on the table for her husband and a mother of a lot of children…twelve in fact. I wanted to become a large animal veterinarian and run my own Animal Clinic. I wanted to drive a really big truck, live in the country, garden, and ride horses any time I wanted. I also wanted to dress up in elegant evening wear and go to 5-star restaurants and dance the night away. I dreamed of traveling and seeing the wonders of the world, meeting interesting people, and experiencing different cultures. I had this deep desire to positively impact the world.

With an innocent naivety, I thought that the universe would align and all my dreams would magically fall into place. After all, that is what happened in the romance novels I devoured and lost myself in. That is also what all the self-improvement books professed to promise. Sure, there was a little work involved, and of course a small rough patch, but ultimately, I would ride off (on my own horse) into the sunset with my knight in shining armor.

Then, the realities of life began to hit me square in the face…and heart. I became lost. I simply accepted what came my way, often without an awareness or understanding of its impact on my dreams and purpose…much less the incremental deterioration of my value and identity. It took years, but eventually I realized that buried beneath my pain, disappointment, disillusionment, and protective walls I had built, was the one whom I still want to be. She was still there, hungering to be revealed and realized.

I moved back in with my parents in August of 1990 after I had been living and supporting myself for six years in Grand Junction, Colorado. I had some amazing experiences. I also had some that were not so great. I met some incredible people and others who, through their own personal wounds and struggles, did some damage to my being. The damage caused me to put up walls around my heart, keeping people at arm's length. I yearned for closeness of relationship, but feared the pain and disappointment that, I came to believe, was inevitable.

I wanted to succeed at something because I felt I was failing at everything. I tried to become what I needed to become to do what I felt like I was supposed to. It simply did not work. Nuggets of truth and a level of wisdom sustained me, but nothing settled me. The psychology, how to succeed in life, business and love/relationship books, and programs did not touch the essence of being a woman hidden beneath the layers of walls disillusionment and disappointment had built.

I will unpack more of my life throughout this book. I do feel though you need to know a few things about me. Overall, I try to be a kind person. I genuinely try to be kind to all people because I believe in the worth of all. I smile at people, even strangers. I am very good at administration. I can look at things from multiple perspectives and see a solution. I have been told I bring order to chaos. I am determined, thrive at a challenge, enjoy proving people wrong when they say I cannot do something. I am a hard worker. I tend to put others first. I enjoy watching people enjoying gatherings. I crave peace, and I love quietness.

I tend to lead, but I can also follow. I am not afraid of a challenge or taking on new things. I do not like to confront but I will if I must. I am not very quick on my feet; I am more of a ponderer. I have very strong beliefs, and I no longer compromise on my core ones. I respect others' right to their opinions, even if they differ from mine. I set very high standards for myself, and I still want to achieve great things. I love to dress up and look pretty. I am very comfortable in my quite unsexy overalls, and I am handy with a chainsaw.

I have wrestled with low-confidence, self-esteem, and have lost myself in an effort to make others happy. I have wrecked good relationships, and I have done very foolish things chasing after bad ones. I have yielded my personhood in the name of conditional love, acceptance, and validation. I have been raped. I have been dumped after engagements and before a wedding day. I have gone through a divorce. And I chose abortion instead of life.

I have been through sexual harassment, sexual discrimination and called colorful adjectives in the workplace. I have been passed over for promotions, even though I was already doing the job. I have also been told that I did not get a job because I was a woman. I have been told what my place is, even though it went against my abilities and sense of fulfillment. I have often felt like I an outsider looking in. I struggle with desiring to be in the limelight but knowing the price it would cost me, I may not be willing to pay. I tried being in control of everything and learned the hard way that control, outside of my own actions, is an illusion.

I have wrestled with what it means to be a woman. I tried to be assertive, loud, demanding. I found it exhausting. I tried to be quiet, hidden, submissive. I found it unsatisfying. Both extremes wailed against the internal voice telling me those are not who I am. I searched for my knight in shining armor, but have since learned that I deserved a prince.

I am a wife, mother, and grandmother. I am content with the person I have become while pursuing the person I will become. I am at peace with my past, and I look forward to my future. It has been quite the journey.

In 1995, I began to study what it means to be a Woman and who God made men to be. It made logical sense to me to start with the creation of Woman. If you do not believe in religion, creation, or God, **do not stop reading.** One, I am not religious, but I am a follower of Jesus Christ. Yes, there is a difference. Two, you were created. You were created with an incredible identity, purpose, and glory that is unique to Womanhood. Three, there is a God, and He loves you. It is not my job to convince you of this; He is more than capable of doing it Himself.

The beauty, wisdom, and strength of Womanhood is extraordinary. But its glorious essence has been diminished, hijacked, distorted, and perverted. Not just by men, but, heartbreakingly, by women too. Women are a force to be reckoned with. Women are mighty, and we are powerful. Women are the carriers of life, strength, and incredible wisdom. Women can also be dangerous and destructive when there is an empty place in our being.

It is time for women to rise in the wonder, beauty, power, and purpose of who we truly are. Not an adapted, forced, or manipulated version of Womanhood, but in the exquisite elegance, magnificence, intelligence, world-changing mystery of being…Woman.

Behold, the Beauty of Woman!

Your Fellow Sister,
Tracy
Up-Word@Outlook.com

Instructions

I have written Behold as a workbook contained within a book. Each chapter takes a topic, breaks it down, and hopefully gives you new information or deepens your current understanding. Then, at the end of each chapter, questions are provided to encourage you to process through the information. You can do this on your own, or with a group.

The beginning of Behold will lay the foundation of who we are as Woman. It is the essence of who Woman is — a reflection of glory. From that foundation, we are to live boldly and confidently in our womanhood accomplishing the purpose we are launched into. We will get into the struggles we have as women, the war against us, our strengths and weaknesses, and the challenges they both bring. Finally, it is my intent that we all engage more fully in our womanhood to accomplish the incredible purpose only women can fulfill.

I will spend a bit of time in the first three chapters of Genesis. If you do not believe in God or Creation, please, again, do not stop reading. I believe the information provided will give you some insight into some of the questions you have been asking yourself. So, I encourage you to complete what you have started.

If you have been hurt, disappointed, or abused by "church", or a leader in the "church," I am so, so sorry. It is not God's heart, nor will, for abuse. God's intent for the Church is for it to be a safe place of corporate worship and prayer, healing, restoration, support, fellowship, and personal growth. We will discuss the role and importance of Church in an upcoming chapter.

The reason we will spend time in the first three chapters of Genesis is if you gain understanding regarding your origin, then you can begin to answer the "whys" of life. When you understand who, how, and with what purpose you were created for, you understand the why behind internal struggles. When you understand what was set in motion when sin entered the world, you understand why males and females act the way they do. When you understand God's original design, and what He is intent on restoring, you have a better understanding of why things happen the way they do.

Information does not transform into understanding without intentionally processing through it. Understanding does not transform our thoughts or behaviors unless we deliberately choose to apply the new understanding to our lives and live it out.

According to Healthline.com, *"It can take anywhere from 18 to 254 days for a person to form a new habit and an average of 66 days for a new behavior to become automatic."* The timeline depends on the person. So, for transformation, I am a big believer in the work it takes to change from one state to another, whether it is physically, mentally, emotionally and spiritually.

I give definitions of words throughout the chapters. I use **Noah Webster's Dictionary 1828** for several reasons, but the primary reason is because in 1828 definitions had a purity and a clarity about them more so than today (in my opinion). It also provides a Scriptural reference in many of the definitions.

In several chapters I will reference or provide the Hebrew or Greek word. Because of our understanding of English definitions, the English word may not convey the richness, or the intended depth the Hebrew and Greek language does. I do not believe that the Bibles written in English are inaccurate. To be clear, there is only ONE Holy Bible; there are different translations. I do believe information in those translations are conveyed differently. That does not make them inaccurate, just easier, or more helpful for you depending upon your purpose.

For example, the English language only has one word for love, yet there are four unique words of love conveyed in the Greek language: *Eros, Storge, Philia*, and *Agape*. *Eros* is romantic love, *Storge* is family love, *Philia* is friendship love, *Agape* is God's divine love.

The Ancient Hebrew language is read right to left, contains 22 letters, and is pictographic. Therefore, individual letters, elements that comprise the letter, the picture it conveys, and the word all have meaning. There are five Hebrew letters for prefixes to provide additional information. Each letter also has a numeric value which increases the meaning wondrously.

PLEASE *keep in mind*, I cannot do justice to the depths of revelation in the Hebrew language. I will attempt to convey the level of meaning relevant to the hope of this book.

This is the letter *Aleph, alef,* א. It is the first letter in the Hebrew alphabet. Its numerical value is 1. The number 1 symbolizes unity, supremacy, and the oneness of the Godhead (God, Jesus Christ, and the Holy Spirit). It means: 1) Master; 2) teacher; 3) wondrous.

> The little mark at the top right, is another letter, *Yod* (*Yud*). It represents God.
> The little mark at the bottom left is also *Yod*. It represents people who dwell on earth.
> The diagonal mark between the two letters *Yod*, is *Vav*. *Vav* represents mankind's unity with God or our faith, which unites us with God.

There is a lot of meaning in this one letter, and the above is not all of it. I will not take you this deep in each letter, but I wanted to give you a glimpse into the wondrous depths of this revelational language.

I have provided certain Hebrew letters or words in the block form, without the additional emphases many of them contain. This is not to lessen the richness or meaning, but for ease of introduction to the word or ease of image of the information being conveyed.

I will reference a concordance as well. **Strong's Exhaustive Concordance of the Bible** is a resource which provides an index of every word in the King James Version (KJV) of the Holy Bible. It helps dig into the depths of the meaning of the words throughout the Bible. There are online tools to accomplish this, but for me, I love the turning of the pages.

I am not a theologian. I am also not an expert in the Hebrew (Old Testament) or Greek (New Testament) languages. But I am a pursuer of God's Truth, therefore I am always learning and growing.

I do know how to access the resources available to me to gain revelation, understanding, and clarity. I am not a lone ranger either; there is wisdom and accountably in godly counsel from others who desire to learn and study. I highly encourage you to dig into all this yourself. God may reveal something to you that He does not to me. Then, we can all benefit together.

Destinations are wonderful, but do not miss the wonder of the journey!

Chapter 1

The Beginning

Mankind was created. Mankind here means humankind. I am secure enough in my womanhood to utilize gender specific words in their primary/global definition. Mankind did not evolve from an amoeba, ape, missing link, or any other organism the scientific community theorizes. Humans were created. Therefore, you, oh woman, were created.

Mankind, the race or species of human beings.

Created, formed from nothing; caused to exist; produced; generated; invested with a new character; formed into new combinations, with a peculiar shape, constitution, and properties; renewed.

Why is this so important? Every thought is based in a belief, on a foundational principle. From every belief, thoughts, perspectives, opinions, and values are formed. Beliefs are more than a passing fancy. Beliefs are at the core of your being. Beliefs are where you govern your life from. Those beliefs then determine how you view everything. Your foundational principle, your belief, on where humankind came from influences how you value yourself, others, and everything in life.

Belief, A persuasion of the truth, or an assent of mind to the truth of a declaration, proposition or alleged fact, on the ground of evidence, distinct from personal knowledge.

Belief that Mankind, over millions of years, evolved from an ape reduces the intrinsic value of Mankind. It categorizes Mankind as less than who we are. Mankind, male and female, was created. We did not evolve from apes; we evolve in our humanness.

You were not only created. You were created in the image of God. Within your DNA, in your attributes, essence and nature, you reflect the image of God. Before you think God is a woman, man is also created in the image of God. Man and Woman, Male and Female reflect God. We each carry similar and unique attributes of the Creator. You were also created in the image of Jesus Christ and the Holy Spirit.

"And God said, Let us make man in our image, after our likeness: and let them have dominion..." (Genesis 1:26a, KJV)

"And God said,"

God is the one who desired and initiated the creation of Mankind. It was through His Word, His absolute power, creative ability and all-encompassing authority, humankind was created.

God is Sovereign. He is the Creator. Within His Creation, God set in place laws, governing principles, and covenants. The Universe, all of creation, and Mankind are subject to these God-ordained functionalities. Mankind can fight against them; however, it will not negate the Truth of how God designed Creation to operate. God created Mankind with the ability to reason and the freewill to choose. Mankind can either work with God, or work against Him. God will always prevail.

"Let Us"

The word "Us" is plural. The plural is God, the Father and Creator; Jesus Christ, the Son, Redeemer, and coming King; and the Holy Spirit, the Teacher, Helper and Comforter.

"make man"

Make, Hebrew: עָשָׂה, *âsâh,* pronounced *aw-saw,* to do, accomplish, advance, appoint, become, bear, bestow, **bring forth** (Strong's 6213).

Man, Hebrew: אָדָם *âdâm,* pronounced *aw-dawn* a human being, (an individual or the species, Mankind) (Strong's 120). The use of the word "man" in this verse has its origins in *âdam, aw-dam* means to show blood, (in the face) flush or turn rosy: be made red (ruddy) (Strong's 119).

So, God, Jesus Christ, and the Holy Spirit **brought forth** Mankind, a **new** species. You did not evolve from an already created one. You are created unique!

"in Our image,"

"Our," again is plural: The Father, Son, and Holy Spirit.

Image, Hebrew: צֶלֶם *tselem,* pronounced *tseh-lem,* a shade, a phantom, illusion, **resemblance;** hence, **a representative** figure (Strong's 6754).

You, through a spiritual personality and moral likeness, resemble God the Father, Jesus Christ, and the Holy Spirit. You were designed to be His representative!

"after our likeness:"

I want to focus on the seemingly insignificant word, *after,* for a moment. Genesis 1:21-25 reads:

> *"And God created great whales, and every living creature that moveth, which the waters brought forth abundantly, **after their kind,** and every winged fowl **after his kind**: and God saw that it was good.*
>
> *And God blessed them, saying, Be fruitful, and multiply, and fill the waters in the seas, and let fowl multiply in the earth. And the evening and the morning were the fifth day.*
>
> *And God said, Let the earth bring forth the living creature **after his kind**, cattle, and creeping thing, and beast of the earth **after his kind**: and it was so. And God made the beast of the earth **after his kind,** and cattle **after their kind,** and every thing that creepeth upon the earth **after his kind**: and <u>God saw that it was good.</u>"* (KJV, emphasis added)

God created this earth, the land and its seas, to sustain life. He created the grass, herbs, and fruit trees with their seeds within themselves to yield more after its kind (verses 1:10-20).

He created every creature, even the creepy crawling things, to bring forth their kind. The whales bring forth other whales that resemble…monkeys? NO! Whales bring forth other whales. Not only did He create them to bring forth their kind, He blessed them and spoke forth, *"be fruitful and multiply, fill the waters and the earth."* God is the original environmentalist.

Conservation and protection of this planet is NOT in conflict with being a follower of Jesus Christ. In fact, it is part of our identity and our purpose. So, do not let it be a source of division. This, and other seemingly sources of conflict with Christianity, becomes less divisive when we understand God's original design of and for us.

God, Jesus Christ, and the Holy Spirit brought you forth *after their likeness, after their kind*! Then, God mandated and blessed us to keep producing other little humans that reflect our kind—which is still in their likeness.

The intrinsic value of every life!

"let them have dominion"

"Them" is not referring to just the male. Nor is it referring to just the female. God mandated, *"let them have dominion"*. So, Man and Woman, male and female, were created by God to share the authority and the responsibility that comes with having dominion.

Dominion, Hebrew: רָדָה *râdâh*, pronounced *raw-dad´* is a prim root that means to tread down, subjugate, to prevail against, reign or rule over (Strong's 7287).

God told us what He was giving mankind dominion over. It was the fish, birds, cattle, over all the earth, and every creeping thing that creeps on the earth. He *never* said to have dominion, to tread down, subjugate, prevail against, reign, or rule over each other.

Males were not given dominion to rule females. Females were not given dominion to rule males. The reason for the warring between male and female comes later. But it was not God's original design for males and females to be at odds with each other. Males and females were meant to share in the ruling over the earth. We were each meant to play a part in the blessing of Creation to be fruitful and multiply.

> *"So God created man in his own image, in the image of God created he him; male and female created he them."* (Genesis 1:27, KJV)

You are created in the image and the likeness of Almighty God!

Chapter 1

Reflection

1. How does knowing Mankind was created, caused to exist, invested with a new character, and formed into a new combination make you feel?
_____
_____
_____
_____
_____

2. How does it change how you view and value yourself?
_____
_____
_____
_____
_____

3. How does knowing Mankind was created elevate how you view others?
_____
_____
_____
_____

4. Write down how knowing Mankind was created changes or reinforces your belief towards the uniqueness of every human?
_____
_____
_____
_____
_____

5. God created the habitat, the environment, for Mankind before He created Mankind. He created an environment for Mankind to flourish and thrive in. Write down a few thoughts about what this says about God and His care for Mankind.

_____
_____
_____
_____
_____

6. After God Himself created the earth, its seasons, and brought forth animals, birds and crawling things, He said, *"Let us make man in our image, after our likeness,"* The Father, the Son, Jesus Christ, and the Holy Spirit of the Living God were involved in our creation. Write down how this makes mankind unique in the creation process.

_____
_____
_____
_____
_____

7. You were made in the image of God. You bear His, Jesus Christ's, and the Holy Spirit's likeness. Think about what that means and write down your thoughts regarding your image and your likeness being that of the Father, Son, and Holy Spirt.

_____
_____
_____
_____
_____

8. God gave both male and female dominion over the things of earth and all it contained. How does this reflect His desire for male and female to exist and function together?

_____
_____
_____
_____
_____
_____

9. Did God ever give the male or female dominion over each other or any other human being? Write down why this is important for you to know.

_____
_____
_____
_____

10. What does this say about the heart of God and the equality of responsibility He gives males and females?

_____
_____
_____
_____
_____

Other Revelations:

_____
_____
_____
_____
_____
_____
_____
_____
_____
_____
_____
_____
_____
_____
_____

Chapter 2

By God's Design

God did not create male and female in His own image to lollygag around doing nothing. He created them with purpose. He also created them with the ability to accomplish their purpose. Therefore, you were created with a purpose, and you were created with the abilities to accomplish your purposes within the overarching purpose of God. Your purposes may change during different seasons of your life. That is one of the wonders of God, seasons.

> *"Then God **blessed** them, and God said to them, "Be **fruitful** and **multiply**; **fill** the earth and **subdue** it; have **dominion** over the fish of the sea, over the birds of the air, and over every living thing that moves on the earth." (Genesis 1:28, emphasis added)*

"Then God blessed them," God certainly seems to enjoy blessing.

Blessed, to pronounce a wish of happiness to one; to express a wish or desire of happiness; to make successful; to prosper in temporal concerns; to set apart or consecrate to holy purposes; to make and pronounce holy; to praise; to magnify; to extol, for excellencies.

You are blessed and you are meant to be continually blessed by God. Blessing and being blessed by God is through relationship as our continued study will reveal.

The Purpose Revealed:

- *Be Fruitful*, Hebrew: *pârâh*, pronounced, *paw-raw,* prim root, to bear fruit, branch off, **bring forth** (fruit), (be, cause to be, make), fruitful, grow, **increase** (Strong's 6509).

We have seen "bring forth" before. It is in Genesis 1:26 when God brought forth Mankind. Our purpose is to bring forth the things of God. Mankind cannot make something from nothing as God can. However, we can bring things forth because God says so. To be fruitful is to increase, to grow, to flourish in the things you do. Flourish is an amazing blessing. God blessed Mankind to open, expand enlarge, to shoot out, to thrive, and be prosperous in the work He has for us.

- *Multiply,* Hebrew: *râbâh*, pronounced, *raw-baw,* prim root, **to increase (in whatever respect),** bring in abundance, be in authority, bring up, continue, enlarge, excel, exceedingly (Strong's 7235).

Humankind is blessed and instructed to increase. This word multiply is not just referring to having children. It is to excel in whatever respect…in revelation, understanding, knowledge, healthy relationships. God desires for humanity to multiply in every area of life.

- *Fill* the earth, the word fill is *replenish* in the King James Version. Hebrew: *mâlê* pronounced *maw-lay,* or *mâlâ* pronounced *maw-law,* a prim root, to fill or be full of, in a wide application, accomplish, confirm, consecrate (Strong's 4390).

Consecrate means to make or declare to be sacred, set apart, dedicated, devote, to the service and worship of God.

Everything that Humankind did was meant to replenish the earth to make it ongoing and sustainable. What we "fill" the earth with was and is meant to be an act of honor to the Lord. and it was meant to confirm that all God created was good, and it was to be consecrated as sacred.

Every act, every work, every child, and every generation is to be considered valuable, treasured, and worthy. Humankind was not created to just fill the earth with arbitrary things and more stuff, but with things that represent the wonder and beauty of God's design and His creation. These acts of service would sustain the fullness of life God designed.

- *Subdue* it, Hebrew: *kâbash*, pronounced, *kaw-bash,* a prim root, to tread down, to conquer, subjugate, bring into subjection (Strong's 3533).

This sounds confusing until you understand what God delegated Mankind to accomplish. God purposed Mankind to master the earth by conquering anything in the earth not aligned with God's design and put it in order with His design. God is telling Mankind that anything that brings destruction or death, trample it out so life can come forth.

God gave males and females the purpose and the authority to accomplish this.

Unfortunately, Mankind throughout history has chosen to tread upon the earth and its inhabitants in pursuit of personal gain, rather than the collective well-being of all which is found in God's design. God has continually counteracted these acts through those who choose to bring forth God's Kingdom, rather than their personal kingdoms.

- Have *dominion*, as stated in Chapter 1, dominion is to rule over, to prevail. Again, God never instructed Mankind to have dominion over other people.

God's purpose, "*…Be **fruitful** and **multiply**; **fill** the earth and **subdue** it; have **dominion**…*", is a joint rulership by males and females. Each created in the image and likeness of God, Jesus Christ, and the Holy Spirit. Each carrying similar and unique attributes of the Creator, that together present a fuller likeness of the whole. Both containing distinctive characteristics designed to work together to accomplish the same purpose…to bring forth the beauty of life.

Oh, the wonder of God's design!

> *"And on the seventh day God ended His work which He had done, and He rested on the seventh day from all His work which He had done. Then God blessed the seventh day and sanctified it, because in it He rested from all His work which God had created and made." (Genesis 2:2-3)*

God blessed the seventh day. The seventh day is referred to as the Sabbath. The day of rest is another wondrous beauty of God's design.

God worked; He was fruitful. He instructed Mankind to work, be fruitful. God multiplied; He increased the inhabitants of the earth. He instructed Mankind to multiply, to increase. God filled the heavens and the earth with wondrous things. He instructed Mankind to keep replenishing what God had started. God subdued the formless earth, its void, and darkness and brought everything into His Light and glorious order. God instructed Mankind to continue to subdue the earth and bring anything that was out of order, into God's ordained order.

God, the Father, gave us, His children, the perfect role model…Him. He later gives us another One to model our lives after.

Then, God rested, and He consecrated and sanctified the completion of His Creative Work. Mankind is to do the same.

God's original design included rest. A day blessed, set aside, to enjoy the fruits of our labor. Humankind, overall, tends to work seven days a week. In the name of productivity and getting ahead, once-in-a-lifetime memories and healthy families have been stolen. Relationships, goodness, joy, kindness, and gentleness have been killed in the illusive pursuit of validation and worth through mankind's perspective of promotion and more. And the toil on our minds, bodies, and spirit has destroyed lives.

> *"And the Lord God formed man of the dust of the ground, and breathed into his nostrils the breath of life; and man became a living soul.* (Genesis 2:7, KJV)

"breathed into" Hebrew: *nâphach*, pronounced *naw-fakh,* prim root, to puff, to inflate, blow hard, scatter, kindle, expire, cause to lose life, seething, snuff (Strong's 5301).

"breath of life" Hebrew: *neshâmâh*, pronounced *nesh-aw-maw'* wind, angry or **vital breath**, **divine inspiration**, intellect; an animal blast, breath, **inspiration, soul, spirit** (Strong's 5397, emphasis added).

The LORD God breathed into man. There is an intimacy in the creation of man that is not recorded in any other aspect of creation. God said all that was created was good. But with man, there is an intimacy of relationship. The act of giving someone mouth-to-mouth resuscitation, the lifesaving, sacrificial act of breathing into someone to restore them to life, is an intimate act. You are breathing into them a part of you.

God breathed into man, *"the breath of life;"* His breath of life and man became *"a living soul."* This act reflects the desire of God for relationship with man and the design of relationship between God and man.

Man is a living soul. The soul is the spiritual, rational, and immortal substance in man. It enables man to think, reason, and gives man the ability to govern self. A soul is also the reason man must have God. God has put eternity in our hearts that beckons our souls. Without God, our souls progress from empty, to bitter, to anger, then ultimately, filled with hate. God is the only One who can fill our souls and make us whole.

> *"The Lord God planted a garden eastward in Eden, and there He put the man whom He had formed."* (Genesis 2:8)

"The Lord God planted a garden," God did the work. He planted and established a garden. This garden had some type of hedge about it to protect and defend what was inside the garden. It was a place where God could position man to flourish and have purpose.

But that is not all this garden was. The word Eden means, *pleasure, delight…to live voluptuously.* Voluptuous, in this context, means luxuriously, with free indulgence of the *purity* of pleasure.

God did not *"put"* man haphazardly in Eden. God appointed and deliberately set in place Man within a hedged in, delightful environment where man could indulge his senses while tending it.

Yes, tending…God designed man to work.

But it was never God's intent for work to define man or validate his worth. Work was and is intended to give us purpose, to develop our intellect, giftings and creatively. Work brings a sense of fulfillment, and when done well, an amazing sense of accomplishment. Work, by God's design, was also meant to bring a sense of contentment, joy and overall well-being.

God, above all, intended work to be done WITH Him, in cooperation with His purpose. Work was never intended to be done without Him.

He is the Source from whom everything flows.

Chapter 2

Reflection

God designed males and females to work; not just to work for no reason, but for and with a purpose.

1. How does this change your view about work?
___
___
___
___

God blessed "them," both male and female. Read the definition of blessing again.

2. What does God blessing humanity say to you about the heart and character of God?
___
___
___
___

3. How does the fact that God blessed humanity when He created them change how you view yourself?
___
___
___
___

4. What do you need to do to continually remind yourself that God, our Creator, desires to bless?
___
___
___
___

Imparted into our being is the purpose to be fruitful, multiply, fill the earth, subdue environments, and have dominion. Take an inventory of your life. Remember, what you put into your life is what you will get out of it.

5a. Is your life *fruitful*? Do not do a comparison to others in the sense of… "well, I am more fruitful than that person."

_____
_____

5b. What type of fruit are you bringing forth in your life? _____
Is good fruit evident?

_____
_____

5c. Are you bringing forth good and attractive characteristics in your life?

_____
_____

5d. Are you bringing forth good things in other people's lives?

_____
_____
_____
_____

6a. How are you *multiplying* in beneficial areas of your life?

_____
_____
_____
_____

6b. Are you increasing in the things that glorify God and bring you joy? _____
How so?

_____
_____
_____
_____
_____

6c. How are you multiplying in areas that benefit others and your community?

_____
_____
_____
_____

6d. If you are not multiplying in areas that benefit others and your community, where could you start to make that a part of your life?

_____
_____
_____

7a. How does your life *fill* the earth? Ask yourself, are you filling your corner of the world with accomplishments that point to the goodness of God?

_____
_____
_____

7b. Do you fill the earth with sacred, beautiful, wonderful things in the service and worship of God?

_____
_____
_____
_____

How?

_____
_____
_____

7c. Is what you fill the world around you with sustainable for those who come after you?

_____
_____
_____
_____
_____

7d. If not, what steps could you take so they would become sustainable?

8a. How do you subdue the environments you are in? Do you bring peace? Do you contribute to the chaos?

8b. When you see a wrong being committed, what is your response?

8c. How do you confront what you know is wrong? Do you stomp your foot and scream? Or do you ignore it and say that it is someone else's responsibility? Be honest in your evaluation of your response.

9. Do you have dominion over your life in the way that God intended dominion to be carried out? How is dominion reflected in your life?

God blessed and gave these instructions to males and females.

10a. Do you try to co-labor with others?
_____
_____
_____
_____
_____

10b. Or do you insert yourself and try to control others? There is a difference between leading with godly authority and controlling.
_____
_____
_____
_____

God rested.

11a. How often do you take time to rest?
_____
_____

11b. How often do you take the time to celebrate and rest at the accomplishment of a task or goal?
_____
_____

11c. Are you so busy doing life you do not enjoy life? Write down some tangible steps towards you taking a day of rest and times of rest.
_____
_____
_____
_____
_____
_____

In your things-to-do list, in your steps to accomplish a goal, include times of rest to be in God's presence and to enjoy the process. If you do not write it down as a part of the process, you will most likely not do it. Learn to Breathe!

12. God breathed into man. We have the breath of God within us which made us a living soul. How does this set you apart and validate your worth?

_____
_____
_____
_____
_____

13. A soul is the reason man must have God. What do you think about this?

_____
_____
_____
_____
_____

14. When we deny God, or rebel against His commands, what do you think the impact on our soul is?

_____
_____
_____
_____

15. The Lord God did the work to create a protected, blissful, cooperative environment for man. God is the same yesterday, today and forevermore. So, what do you think God's heart for your environment to be is?

_____
_____
_____
_____
_____
_____
_____

The Garden which God put man in was called Eden, which means delight, bliss, indulgence of the senses.

16a. What was God's hope for man when He placed man in the Garden?
_____
_____
_____

16b. What do you think God's hope for you is?
_____
_____
_____
_____

God put, He positioned, man in the Garden to tend and keep it.

17a. How does this purpose *"to tend and keep"* translate to us today?
_____
_____
_____
_____

17b. What do you think God wants you to tend and keep?
_____
_____
_____
_____

Other Revelations:
_____
_____
_____
_____
_____
_____

Chapter 3

Bliss

The Garden of Eden was God's perfect environment for mankind to enjoy, flourish and have purpose. God created it and positioned man in it.

> *"And out of the ground made the Lord God to grow every tree that is pleasant to the sight, and good for food; the tree of life also in the midst of the garden, and the tree of knowledge of good and evil."* (Genesis 2:9, KJV)

God started everything. God's desire for mankind was to continue and care for what He had started. The continuation of the work was meant to be in one-on-one relationship with Him. This is important to understand that God created mankind for relationship. God's intent was that He and man would be in constant relationship. They would do the work together.

> *"the tree of life also in the midst of the garden,"*

God planted the Tree of Life right in the middle of His Masterpiece. It was the centerpiece of this luxurious environment. God is intentional, never haphazard. The Tree of Life being planted in the middle of the Garden was a living reminder that Life is the Source of all things. Life is what everything else flows from. If Life is not the centerpiece of your life, then your life will not flow as it was designed to flow.

> *"And a river went out of Eden to water the garden; and from thence it was parted, and became into four heads."* (Genesis 2:10, KJV)

I want to take a little road-less-traveled trip with you. Read Genesis 2:10 again. On its surface it seems to be simply conveying information about how God watered Eden, and then the river traveled out of the Garden and became four rivers. *River*, when you look it up in Strong's, means a stream, figuratively, prosperity. It is from the prim root of *nâhar*, to sparkle, be cheerful, to flow, be lightened (Strong's 5104 and 5102). There is more than just a water source being conveyed.

A river represents life. Without a river, a water source, life withers and will ultimately die. God created a river that started in a place of bliss, then divided it into four other rivers. From one source of life, four additional suppliers of life were born. Their origins will always lead back to the Source. The number four speaks to God's creative ability. In four days, God had created the material universe. In the Bible, the number four indicates completeness. And the fourth commandment is the Sabbath rest, which rest is needed for meaningful and healthy life.

In John 7:38, Jesus Christ, who is the way, the truth, and the LIFE, tells us, *"He who believes in Me, as the Scripture has said, out of his heart will flow rivers of living water."*

How FUN is that?! The Word of God is not boring. The more you read, study, and meditate on the Holy Bible, the deeper and richer it gets. The Word of God brings life. The revelation of His Word explodes joy inside of you! You will be blessed if you just scratch the surface. That is just the power of God's Word. But, oh, the treasures you will discover if you dig a little deeper.

The Tree of Life was planted in the center of the Garden. The Tree of Knowledge of Good and Evil was also in the midst of the Garden. There is more on this Tree in Chapter 6.

> *"And the Lord God took the man, and put him into the garden of Eden to dress it and to keep it."* (Genesis 2:15, KJV)

"to dress" Hebrew: *âbad*, pronounced *aw-bad*, prim root, to work (in any sense), **to serve**, till, **enslave**, keep in bondage, bring to pass, (set a) work, **worshipper** (Strong's 5647, emphasis added).

AND,

"to keep" Hebrew: *shâmar*, pronounced *shaw-mar*, prim root, **to hedge about,** to guard, **protect, be circumspect**, take heed (to self), keep, **look narrowly**, observe, **preserve**, wait for, **watch** (Strong's 8104, emphasis added).

Before every part of your being rebels against the meanings of *"dress"* and *"keep,"* let us put them in the proper context.

God put the man in a place of BLISS! God gave man the responsibility to serve, to be enslaved (passionate) to this glorious delight of God. Man was to keep God's creation in order. Man was to do these things with God as a worshipper of God. This created the perfect situation to maintain a beautiful, intimate, personal relationship by working together to accomplish amazing things and care for a wondrous creation.

God also gave the man the responsibility to set a hedge about the Garden, to guard and protect it. Man was to be prudent and watchful on ALL sides. He was to be circumspect, his head swiveling in all directions. He was to carefully examine all aspects of a circumstance. Have you ever seen something and wondered at it? You look narrowly at it. You squint your eyes, lower your head, move closer to take a better look to determine what it is. You wait and watch what it does, you observe how it acts, then you take all the information and decide how to proceed.

God created man with the ability to be aware of his surroundings and the intellect to respond to situations wisely.

God authorized man to dress and keep His Delight. God made man…a gardener!

God gave man further instructions on his role and his responsibilities.

> *"And the Lord God commanded the man, saying, '"Of every tree of the garden you may freely eat; but of the tree of the knowledge of good and evil you shall not eat, for in the day that you eat of it you shall surely die.'"* (Genesis 2:16-17)

Today, in a world of *you can't tell me what to do*, we are not thrilled at the word command. We also put God in an angry, control freak, have-no-fun category because we view the word command negatively. I am going to reiterate, God is Sovereign. He is all powerful and He is all knowing. He can, in a single moment, wipe out humanity and the entire world.

He is also just. He is the God of justice. It was evident in the Old Testament, New Testament, and will continue to be in the coming days. There will be a Day of Judgment where every human will give an account of their life. We will be judged by a righteous and holy Judge. There is no debating nor disputing this Truth. You, sooner or later, will need to settle this truth resolutely within yourself.

But…His heart, His desire, is extraordinarily evident in His continual plea for Mankind to abide with Him and live in a blessed state.

So, when God commanded man not to eat of the Tree of Knowledge of Good and Evil, God was protecting man. But He was not taking away man's responsibility to reason, to narrowly look at something, and decide for himself. You cannot blame God for man's choosing outside of God's commands.

Commanded, Hebrew: *tsâvâh*, pronounced, *tsaw-vaw*, to constitute (to set, fix, enact, establish), enjoin, appoint, give a charge, send with a command, send a messenger, **put (set) in order** (Strong's 6680, emphasis added).

God enacted, established, a boundary for the good of man. The man was appointed and sent with the command do not eat from the Tree of Knowledge of Good and Evil. He was given the responsibility to be the messenger to others about the consequences of knowing good and evil. Man was meant to protect others from the dangers of disobeying God. God put things in order; man was given the charge to keep them in order according to God's design.

What about the woman? She is coming because man is not presenting a complete picture. *"It is not good for him to be alone."* If man was presenting a complete picture of something, then there would be no need for woman to come into being. But this does not mean that man himself was incomplete. It was stating it is not good for man, people, to be alone. God was revealing a picture of someone else.

> *"And the Lord God said, It is not good that the man should be alone; I will make him an help meet for him."* (Genesis 2:18, KJV)

We need to have a truthful understanding of God's design of male, female, the original environment, and His heart for us. We need to understand where we came from, who we are meant to be, and where God is pointing us towards. There is wonder in being male, and there is wonder in being female…we have similarities, but we are unique in the individual glories of masculinity and femininity.

Without both represented, there is an incomplete picture. The fullness of glory is found in the beauty of the masculine and feminine working together.

> *"Out of the ground the Lord God formed every beast of the field and every bird of the air and brought them to Adam to see what he would call them. And whatever Adam called each living creature, that was its name. So Adam gave names to all cattle, to the birds of the air, and to every beast of the field. But for Adam there was not found a helper comparable to him."* (Genesis 2:19-20)

"and brought them to Adam (man)" God, once again, doing the lion-share of the work brought every beast and every bird to Adam, *"to see what he would call them."*

Why did God bring the animals to Adam? It seems like it would be easier for God to tell Adam, "This is a horse." But that is not whom God created Adam to be.

God was further establishing Adam in his identity as God's representative on earth. God was also commissioning Adam to accomplish his purpose! God could have done it all. Yet, He chose to delegate responsibility to Adam. Why?

To set things in order.

God positioned Adam. Adam positioned what God had created. That is one very close working relationship.

"to see what he would call them"

"to see", this is another one of those seemingly insignificant words we tend to gloss over. This word "see" reveals another aspect of the wonder that is God.

See, Hebrew: *râ'âh*, pronounced, *raw-aw*, prim root, to see…advise, appear, approve, behold, (make to) enjoy, **have experience**, gaze, take heed, **indeed joyfully**, **to look upon one another**, meet, be near, have regard, **have respect** (Strong's 7200, emphasis added). We are talking about God's response.

Almighty God brought HIS creation to Adam, so He, the Creator of the Universe, could share the experience with Adam, JOYFULLY. God and Adam during every encounter carrying out the work that needed to be accomplished, they looked upon each other, and had regard and respect for one another. Every experience was made to be ENJOYED!

Is that not simply wondrous!?

Call, Hebrew: *qârâ'*, pronounced, *kaw-raw*, to call out, to proclaim (Strong's 7121).

God anointed Adam to call out, to proclaim, who each animal was. Adam was carrying out his purpose, WITH GOD, to position God's creatures.

Name, Hebrew: *shêm,* pronounced, *shame,* definite and conspicuous position, an appellation (the word by which a thing is called and known), **a mark of individuality**, by honor, authority, character (Strong's 8034, emphasis added).

Adam did not carelessly name God's creation. He utilized His being *"to dress and to keep"* what had been charged to him. He looked narrowly at each species, their form and function, and he named them to set them in their identity and purpose.

Each creature was given *a mark of their individuality* by Adam, face to face with, and at the pleasure and great joy of God.

The importance of what God and Adam accomplished together carries through to today. When I think of a horse, I do not envision a dog. I see in my mind the unique characteristics of a horse, the beauty, grace, and strength. I see them running, with their manes streaming, hooves thundering…the thought brings a smile to my face.

The power to call and to name is still man's responsibility today. Its importance has not diminished.

A man is to proclaim and position...sharing the experience WITH GOD!

When man chooses to proclaim and position without God, identities are skewed, and destinies are not established in God's order. Destruction follows in its wake. A wounded man, or a man who has not been shown better will declare wounded and hurtful words over those he encounters. I am not justifying the behavior. I am, hopefully, opening hearts and minds to an understanding so healing can take place in your life.

When a father calls a son a failure, failure becomes a part of the son's identity and sets him on a path of failure. When a man calls a woman a derogatory name, the name infiltrates a woman's identity and sets her on a path to fulfill that name. Woman, you are not off the hook, for the same applies to women. There are too many songs, shows, games, advertisements, etc. degrading men and women. Those, and spoken words, are knowingly and unknowingly diminishing the worth of every human. Thank the Lord for the power to restore and redeem lives.

It is the purpose of men to call out, to proclaim, to set into position. It is also men's purpose to protect, to dress and to keep what God has entrusted them with.

Chapter 3

Reflection

The Garden of Eden was God's perfect environment for man to enjoy, flourish, and have purpose.

1. How would this translate to today, specifically in your life?

_____
_____
_____
_____
_____
_____

God planted the Tree of Life in the middle of the Garden.

2a. Why is this significant?

_____
_____
_____
_____
_____
_____

2b. What importance does it have in your life today?

_____
_____
_____
_____
_____
_____
_____

God also planted the Tree of Knowledge of Good and Evil in the Garden.

3. Why do you think that was?
_____
_____
_____

4. What do you think is the significance of the Tree of Knowledge of Good and Evil?
_____
_____
_____
_____

5. Why did God tell man not to eat of this tree?
_____
_____
_____
_____
_____

A river flowed through the Garden, then divided into four other rivers.

6. Why do you think this was important enough to mention in the Holy Bible?
_____
_____
_____
_____

The Lord God, *"put man in the Garden of Eden to dress it and to keep it."*

God positioned man in God's delight, a place of Bliss.

7a. What is this act of God saying to you?
_____
_____
_____
_____

7b. How does it apply to your life today?

God purposed man to be watchful and protect the Garden and all that was in it.

8. What does this say to the purpose of man?

God made man a gardener.

9a. What are some characteristics of gardeners?

9b. What are some of the fruits when a gardener is fruitful?

9c. What are some of the fruits when a gardener does not keep their garden well?

10. When God commanded man to not eat of the fruit from the Tree of Knowledge of Good and Evil, what was God doing?

_____
_____
_____
_____

11. What were some other responsibilities God gave man when He commanded man not to eat from the Tree of Knowledge of Good and Evil?

_____
_____
_____
_____
_____

12. Why do you think God said, *"It is not good that the man should be alone."*

_____
_____
_____
_____

God brought the animals to Adam to call out and to name.

13a. Why do you think God did this in this manner?

_____
_____
_____
_____
_____

13b. Why did He not tell Adam to call out and name the creatures and get back with Him when the task was done?

_____
_____
_____
_____
_____

14. How does God's interaction with Adam reflect God's heart?

15. How would this desire of God to work together with Mankind apply today?

16. How do your words call out and position others in their God-given identities and destinies?

17. Are your words at the pleasure and great joy of God?

Why or why not?

18a. What words has man called you that hurt or hindered your identity (how you see yourself)?

18b. How can you start to find healing and restoration from those words?

_____
_____
_____
_____

19. Woman, are you encouraging men to be the man God has called them to be?

_____
_____
_____
_____
_____
_____

Why or why not?

_____
_____
_____
_____

Other Revelations:

_____
_____
_____
_____
_____
_____
_____
_____
_____
_____
_____
_____

Chapter 4

A Comparable Help Meet

God created a Garden—Eden. He put man in the Garden. Man began to carry out his purpose to dress and keep the Garden. Adam also began to call out and name the living creatures as God brought them to him. But man was alone, and it was not good according to God.

> *"And the Lord God said, It is not good that the man should be alone; I will make him an help meet for him."* (Genesis 2:18, KJV)

God created them male and female in the image of God. He did not create just male in His image. He did not create just female in His likeness. He, Jesus Christ, and the Holy Spirit created male and female to represent their image and likeness on earth.

God also blessed them and said to them, not just him or her, but both to *"be fruitful and multiply: fill the earth and subdue it; and have dominion over every living thing that moves on the earth."* Reminder, He **never** gave male or female dominion over one another.

God made man complete in his identity and in his being as male. Adam was not missing something. He, within himself, lacked nothing. However, God said it is not good *in the wildest sense, beautiful, best, bountiful, cheerful, at ease* for man to do life alone (good, Strong's 2896).

God did not say, I need to make Adam someone who fits a part I messed up on. God, in essence, was saying, I will make someone for Adam who is equal to him, who will help him to carry out My purpose, but carries different attributes. God was providing humanity a revelation that was incomplete by God revealing only Adam. But the personhood, the masculinity, the identity of who Adam was created to be was complete within him.

Alone, Hebrew, *bad*, pronounced *bad*, separation, a part of the body, branch of a tree (Strong's 905). Interesting meaning of alone, is it not? Bad, is from, *bâdâ, baw-daw*, to divide, be solitary (Strong's 909).

It is not good for man to be separated. It is not good for man to be solitary.

Adam, male, presented only part of a picture, much like a part of a body only presents a portion of the whole. A branch presents only part of a tree. You must step back and look at the whole tree to see the full picture…to begin to grasp the full revelation.

In Genesis 1:26-27, God said, *"Let us make **man(kind)** in **Our image,** according to **Our likeness**, let **them**…in the image of God He created him; **male and female** He created them."* (emphasis added)

Male and female TOGETHER present a more complete picture of the image and likeness of God, Jesus Christ, and the Holy Spirit. Our similarities and our unique characteristics together are meant to reflect the fullness of who God is.

Read the definition of "alone" again. It says a part of the body, a branch of a tree. Who is the trunk that holds the branches? The branches cannot sustain life without being connected to the trunk. Mankind cannot sustain life without being genuinely and continually connected to his Source.

Man(kind) has done things in the name of God, but they violate the heart and will of God. Therefore, they are not sincerely connected to God. Religion has used rules and regulations in the name of God, but with God, it is not about religion. It has always been and will always be about relationship…constant connection to Him. The Tree of Life…the Source of Life.

> *"And the Lord God said, It is not good that the man should be alone; **I will make him an help meet for him.** And out of the ground the Lord God formed every beast of the field, and every fowl of the air; and **brought them unto Adam to see what he would call them**: and **whatsoever Adam called every living creature, that was the name thereof**. And Adam gave names to all cattle, and to the fowl of the air, and to every beast of the field; but for Adam there was not found **an help meet for him**."*
> (Genesis 2:18-20, emphasis added, KJV)

Help *meet*, Hebrew: *êzer*, pronounced *ay-zer*, aid, help (Strong's 5828). From *āzar*, pronounced, *aw-zar*, to surround or protect (Strong's 5826).

Aid, to help; to assist; to support, either by furnishing strength or means to effect a purpose, or to prevent or remove evil.

Surround, to encompass; to environ; to enclose on all sides; as, to surround a city.

Protect, to cover or shield from danger or injury; to defend; to guard; to preserve in safety; a word of general import both in a literal and figurative sense.

God created female to aid. Females help, assist, and support by furnishing strength or means (resources) to effect (to produce) a purpose. Females assist to prevent or remove evil. Females enclose on all sides to cover and shield from danger. Females defend, guard, and preserve in safety. These are very powerful attributes God gave females.

Now, before the blood pressure of women blows through the roof, aid, surround, and protect are **NOT** subservient terms. Nor are they dictating males always lead, and females always follow. That was not God's intent. *Ezer* is used 21 times in the Old Testament. It is used for: 1) woman; 2) for nations to whom Israel appealed for military aid, and 3) for God as Israel's helper.

Ezer is, however, a term of order, and within it, a connotation of respect for others. God is not an Author of confusion, but of order. Aid is not something given unless a true need is evident, or it is asked for. Women, we tend to give our opinion to a situation where it is not needed, or it has not been asked for. This means we need to operate in understanding and in wisdom and with boundaries.

Help meet, Hebrew, *ezer kenegdo*, translates to *"power"* or *"strength"*, *"a helper against him"* so in essence, God is saying in Genesis 2:18, "I will make a power or strength equivalent to man."

She will be rendered equal to man, fully his equal, fully his match. Male and female will be parallel to one another, separate but equal. Each carrying similar characteristics yet also unique attributes that define masculinity and femininity. Males and females are like the two sides of the same river, or two sides to the same coin.

A great analogy between male and female is the right and left hands. They are very similar in form and function. Individually, they can accomplish quite a bit. They can, however, accomplish more and with more efficiency when they are working together.

And there are some things that are nearly impossible to accomplish if they are not working together.

*"a helper **against** him"*, This is not contradictory in its meaning. Rabbi Solomon ben Isaac, known as Rashi, an influential Jewish commentator, made this point, *"If he [Adam] is worthy, [she will be] a help [ezer]. If he is not worthy [she will be] against him [kenegdo] for strife."*

This is not talking about Adam's intrinsic worth as man, but worthy as a help meet in the fulfillment of their God-given purpose.

There are stories in the Word of God where Woman stood against Man to either fulfill God's commands or to obtain God's promises. They did not gossip, shout, or stomp their feet. They stated their case, stood their ground, and were found faithful. They also did not achieve their end goal at the expense of a Man having to become less than who God created him to be.

Numbers 27 tells an interesting story of the daughters of Zelophehad. Their father had died in the wilderness, and there was no son to receive the inheritance due to the family. The five daughters stood up in their strength and presented their case before Moses. Moses then took the case before the Lord, and the Lord said that the daughters of Zelophehad were correct. The daughters then took possession of their inheritance. They took a stand against something that was not just. They obtained the promise of God.

If males and females do not operate in their true and healthy identities to work together, they will be in strife against one another. And since both male and females were created with power and strength, strife, ultimately, will bring the destruction of both.

This is NOT God's desire nor design.

The Torah Study for Reform Jews presents a magnificent picture of the relationship between male and female as God desired in creation. They are facing each other, with arms raised, hands pressed together creating an arch between them. It is an incredible illustration of *equal responsibility*, perfectly balanced. If one presses harder, then the other is pushed back. If one walks away, the other falters.

> *"And the Lord God caused a deep sleep to fall on Adam, and he slept; and He took one of his ribs, and closed up the flesh in its place. Then the rib which the Lord God had taken from man He made into a woman, and He brought her to the man."* (Genesis 2:21-22)

God created woman from the rib of man.

I find it interesting that God chose to create woman from the rib of man. God could just as easily formed her from the dust as He did Adam. But God chose a different form of creation to create woman. The rib is an interesting bone. Its attributes and function represent the woman's characteristics. They — the ribs — surround internal organs for protection. They lend strength to support the trunk of the body to facilitate uprightness. They supply the means for the lungs to function. They also provide a place where some muscles originate or attach. They also contribute to the production of red blood cells during development.

In my attempt to grasp understanding of God's creation of female, I picture it this way. God wanted man and woman to be comparable, so they needed to share some characteristics. But they also needed to balance each other, depend upon each other to do their individual part, and each needed to contribute to the overall purpose. So, God "pulled out" certain characteristics of man and formed female. This thought probably would not stand up to theological scrutiny. But it helps me to wrap my mind around the process.

"He brought her to the man" is not an indication by God that woman was incomplete in her femininity. It was also not an indication that she was subservient to man. He brought her to man because that is the PROTOCOL that God set up. God does not violate His own Word. He does not create confusion or chaos by changing the process He set in order.

This becomes quite important as we continue, so keep in mind, God does not violate His own Word.

God presented woman to Adam so He would see what Adam would call her. And, whatever Adam would call her, that would be her name. God was more than capable of naming the woman Himself. However, God did not circumvent what He purposed Adam with.

Adam, operating in his identity and purpose, looked narrowly at the woman, studied her closely, saw her similar and distinct characteristics and called her out and named her.

> *"And Adam said, This is now bone of my bones, and flesh of my flesh: she shall be called Woman, because she was taken out of Man."* (Genesis 2:23, KJV)

The Lord brought, presented, the woman to Adam. Adam named her Woman *(Ishah)* and called out her God-given identity and set in motion her purpose. God created and purposed woman just as He created and purposed man. No one can take that away from either. Our God-given intrinsic worth, identity and purpose can only be relinquished.

Man, *Ish*. Woman, *Ishah*. The first time that Adam is called *Ish* (Man) is when *Ishah* (Woman) is created from him by God

The creation story of Man and Woman implies that male and female cannot fully express each other or humanity without the other…two sides of the same coin. Together, male and female present a more complete picture, the likeness and image, of God.

Oh, the beauty Humanity can press towards.

Chapter 4

Reflection

God said it is *"not good"* for man to be alone.

1a. Why do you think that is?
_____
_____
_____
_____

1b. How does being alone (too much) affect people's well-being?
_____
_____
_____
_____

Alone, means separation, a part of the body, a branch of a tree.

2a. What is the effect of a missing part of the body?
_____
_____
_____
_____

2b. What are the effects of a branch not being connected to the tree?
_____
_____
_____
_____

3. What else was God saying when He said it is not good for man to be alone, separated from the Body?

_____
_____
_____
_____

4. What happens to people when they are separated from the Source of Life?

_____
_____
_____
_____

Help meet, ezer, aid, help, surround or protect.

5. When you read these words regarding what embodies a female, what else comes to your mind?

_____
_____
_____
_____

Aid, to help; to assist; to support, either by furnishing strength or means to affect a purpose, or to prevent or remove evil.

6a. What is this saying about female attributes?

_____
_____
_____
_____

6b. Are you empowering women to embrace these attributes? _____
How?

_____
_____
_____
_____

7. How does a woman aid in the prevention or removal of evil?

_____
_____
_____
_____

Surround, to encompass; to environ; to enclose on all sides; as, to surround a city.

8a. How does a woman "enclose on all sides" someone or something (a purpose for example)?

_____
_____
_____
_____
_____

8b. What are some of the negative sides of "enclosing on all sides"?

_____
_____
_____
_____

Protect, to cover or shield from danger or injury; to defend; to guard; to preserve in safety; a word of general import both in a literal and figurative sense.

A woman, typically, is not physically as strong as a man.

9a. So, how does a woman cover or shield others from danger?

_____
_____
_____
_____

9b. How is a woman to defend, guard and preserve in safety someone or something?

_____
_____
_____
_____

Help meet, Hebrew, *ezer kenegdo*, translates to *"power"* or *"strength"*, *"a helper against him"* so in essence, God is saying in Genesis 2:18, "I will make a power or strength equivalent to man."

10a. What are some positive outcomes of co-laboring with someone who has the power and strength equivalent to you?

_____
_____
_____
_____

10b. What are some of the challenges that can come out of co-laboring with someone who has the power and strength equivalent to you?

_____
_____
_____
_____

> *"a helper against him", "If he [Adam] is worthy, [she will be] a help [ezer]. If he is not worthy [she will be] against him [kenegdo] for strife." — Rashi.*

11. What is the outcome when men and women do not have a healthy understanding of their identity, worth, and purpose?

_____
_____
_____
_____
_____

12. When a husband or wife is not in alignment with their God-given identities, what is the outcome?

_____
_____
_____
_____
_____

13. What is God's desire for male and females co-laboring together (according to the Torah Study for Reform Jews)?

___

God created woman from the rib of man. God is intentional in everything He does.

14. Why do you think He created woman differently than other elements of creation?

___

15a. Does this make her superior?

___

Why or why not?

___

16. Why did God bring the woman to the man?

___

17. What did Adam do when He named the woman, Woman?

___

Men and women are two sides of the same coin or resemble the analogy of the usage of left and right hands.

18. What happens to humanity when males dominate or exclude females, or females dominate or exclude males?

___

19. What was, and is, God's hope and desire for humanity?

___

20. What insight do you gain by understanding God's creation?

___

21. How does it impact how you see yourself and others?

___

22. How does God's design of humanity, male and female, impact how you view God?

Other Revelations:

Chapter 5

In The Presence Of

Man and Woman were created to fulfill God's purpose to, *be fruitful, and multiply, and replenish the earth, and subdue it: and have dominion over it,* in the presence of each other. Most importantly, live in the presence of God Himself.

The fulfillment of God's purpose would be possible through the contributions each one made to the process.

> *"And Adam said, This is now bone of my bones, and flesh of my flesh: she shall be called Woman, because she was taken out of Man."* (Genesis 2:23, KJV)

Adam is never called *Ish* until *Ishah* had been separated from him. Previously, Adam represented a neutral term, human. Man, beginning in this verse, is now called *Ish,* and woman is called *Ishah*. The Old Testament continues to identity *Ish* as man and *Ishah* as woman. Let us look at the names broken down in their pictorial Hebrew form to better understand the power of these words.

Ish (man) איש

    א **Aleph:** Strong, Power, Leader
        To learn, or teach, produce thousands; root means oxen-team up
        Picture portrays the head of an Ox

    י **Yod:** Strength, Hand, Work, Make, Throw, Worship (as in a Warrior)
        Holding something, synonymous with power or might; to fall in one's hands
        A hand, closed or closing, to imply a deed done, or a finished work
        Picture portrays an arm and closed hand

    ש **Shin:** Sharp(en), Tooth or Teeth, Press, Eat, Two
        Represents carefully chewing over something; represents strength (teeth are strong); ability to remain strong regardless of circumstances; changes for the good; return to
        Sharpening of swords, arrows, one's tongue, one's mind (Deuteronomy 6:7)
        Picture portrays sharp teeth

Ishah (woman) אשה

    א **Aleph:** Strong, Power, Leader

    ש **Shin:** Sharp(en), Tooth or Teeth, Press, Eat, Two

    ה **Hey:** Behold, Reveal, Breath, Revelation
        Early Hebrew picture portrayed a man's arm raised, as when you throw your arms up when you behold something wonderful – you are awestruck by the marvel by the sight or revelation
        It is also a picture of an open window, a unique perspective from which to view things

Ish and *Ishah* both begin with *Aleph*, א, strong, power, leader, represented by the ox. Both man and woman were, and are, to learn, teach, to produce thousands…and to team up. Oxen learn how to work together by being yoked together. An older, more experienced, and knowledgeable ox is yoked with an inexperienced one to teach it. Together, the oxen are able to pull significantly more weight than when alone.

The teacher must be willing to teach and have patience. The student must be willing to learn. BOTH must submit to the yoke. The teacher carries the bulk of the work, then gradually transfers the weight to the student until the weight is equally distributed. Then, the student becomes the teacher to another student. This is called mentorship or discipleship. It is also the process to produce and multiply. Sound familiar?

God is the ultimate leader. Man and Woman are to be individually yoked with God first. This is so we can learn about Him and His ways before teaching others. God entrusts us with more and more responsibility as we mature in our understanding of the work He has called us to.

Marriage is the yoke between a man and a woman. They come together to accomplish the MUTUALLY agreed upon purpose of the marriage. Other types of yokes occur when people, of their own accord, come together to accomplish the vision set before them. Being yoked together in God's design was not a subservient, one is more important than the other, design. It is a unity, each contributing their strength to accomplish the overall good. But there is always order.

I daresay there is nothing that can be accomplished completely by oneself. I am sitting here, alone in my office, writing this book. However, I am not doing it completely by myself. I did not create the computer. I access the work of others, I ask others their thoughts, and so on. The contributions of others are assisting me in the accomplishment of my goal. You might say what about someone building a fire with no manmade tools? I would ask, who grew the trees? Humanity needs humanity. But for humanity to function in a healthy manner, humanity needs God. It is not good for humanity to be disconnected from Him.

Ish and *Ishah* both contain *Shin*, שׁ, however, in a different order. This too, is not an indication of less than, simply different in how Man and Woman operate in strength. The letter, *Shin,* comprises three vertical lines, which looked more like teeth in earlier forms. Now, it resembles a crown. The three lines, depending upon the context of its usage, represent:

> The three general dimensions of a person: *emotions; intellect; will and pleasure.*
> Those three dimensions contain three impartations:
> > 1) Will and pleasure contain: *justice; mercy; kindness*
> > 2) Intellect contains: *understanding; application of knowledge; flash of an idea*
> > 3) Emotions contain: *severity or discipline; mercy or compassion; kindness*

I could spend numerous pages diving into the depths of S*hin* and its application to our being. Oh, the treasure-trove of knowledge and understanding revealed in its depths!

Man and Woman were, and are, created with strength and passion. Both have the ability to chew over a matter. Both are created with the ability to remain strong regardless of the circumstances we encounter. Both are created with the capability and the capacity to make changes for the good, internally, and externally. Both are created with the fundamental necessity to always return to God. Without Him, whether we like it or not, we will continually flounder and miss the mark. It is about relationship, not religion.

Man, *Ish* contains *Yod*, י, which encompasses utilizing the hand and arm in work and worship. *Yod* is the smallest letter yet carries quite a meaning. Man is to lend his masculine attribute of strength to the task through utilizing his strength in work and worship. But when *Yod* is not submitted to God's strength, the blessing of strength in work and worship can become the curse of working to be the worshipped.

Yod, is the first letter in God's Sacred Name YHVH (Yahweh). So, this strength, this masculine strength, carries a different connotation. It is used to accomplish the work God gave Man. Work is an act of worship. God gave Man a garden, an environment, to tend and keep. Man, as an act of honoring God for entrusting the care of Creation to him, is meant to carry out his work with diligence and excellence. This carries through to today: Man's work should be an act of worship to God.

Ishah contains *Hey*, ה. *Hey* is a portrayal of a breathtaking reaction to seeing something wondrously revealed. Women are to behold, to look at something, and get insight to accomplish the task with wisdom. It is all about perspective, seeing a situation from a different angle and discerning how to go about it with grace. Women crave knowledge and understanding because it is a part of our design.

Hey is also found in God's Name, YHVH. Woman is divinely connected to God, as is Man. Woman was designed to operate in wisdom. This does not mean Man cannot operate in wisdom. He can. Woman has a unique perspective in operating in wisdom. Woman, through thought, speech, and action, brings wisdom into the accomplishment of the purpose God sets her to. This is Woman's act of work and worship. However, if Woman looks to wisdom as her validation, wisdom becomes an idol, and can be used for the manipulation and control of others. When Woman is secure in her identity, and in relationship with God, wisdom — the revelation she receives — benefits all for good.

Elohim is the Name given for God as Creator. Elohim denotes strength, power, and justice. We have seen strength and power in the attributes of both Man and Woman, *Aleph*.

God's Sacred Name YHVH, *Yod, Hey, Vav, Hey*. Yahweh expresses God's closeness, His intimacy, to humankind: *He breathed into man the breath of life*. It is the intimacy of *Yod* and *Hey*, that contributes to the yearning within humanity for Yahweh, God. Even if humanity tries to deny the deep desire to be connected to someone greater than self.

Vav is a hook, more accurately a connecting hook. *Vav* represents essential connective powers. It suggests the connection between spiritual and earthly matters; it also indicates the creative connection between all the Hebrew letters. *Vav* is the connecting force of Almighty God that binds together heaven and earth. He, not Mankind, holds that power.

There is a consequence when Man and Woman remove Yahweh from their life.

Aleph and *Shin* together mean fire. Man and Woman both carry fire. It can be a fire meant to warm, bring comfort, or to ignite the passion necessary to accomplish a purpose. Fire can also be destructive and can destroy oneself or others. Both are consuming fires; one accomplishes good, the other brings devastation.

If *Yod*, God, who gives the strength to control it, is removed, fire always destroys. So, when Man removes God from His life, his leadership and passion is unrestrained. He serves only himself and will destroy others to accomplish his selfish desires, and an emptiness will remain in his being.

For Woman, when God, who holds all wisdom (Hey), is removed, the wisdom to manage fire properly is skewed. It no longer holds the purity of good and holiness. The leadership and passion of Woman pursues identity, validation, and purpose through a distorted view. She looks to her own interests above all else, regardless of the price others pay in her wake. She twists wisdom to her own advantage, and it ultimately destroys herself and others.

When Man and Woman both remove God from their lives, two uncontrolled fires come together through relationship. This intensifies the strength and passion of both, and they become capable of great destruction. They begin to struggle with dominance over one another. A strong desire to destroy each other rises to the surface, and if a return to God does not occur, destruction will take place. The price of this consuming fire not only burns them but anyone in their sphere of relationship…including children.

God is a consuming fire. It means exactly what it says, God is a consuming fire. God is holy and He does not share His glory with any idol we have in our life, including setting ourselves up as an idol. He will not compete with an idol, and He will not settle for anything in our lives remaining unholy. God's holiness refines our hearts so that every idol is removed, and sin no longer rules our lives. He does this out of His love for us. Because He knows out of proper order priorities hinders us and sin puts us into a bondage.

He will not negate our responsibility to freewill. He does not violate what He has set in order. So, we can continue to choose to worship idols (money, titles, other gods, ourselves), operate continually in sin, rebel ,or even deny His existence. But, know this, there will come a day when His consuming fire will destroy idolatry and rebellion. He is holy. He is just, and He is merciful —which is why He sent Jesus Christ.

We can continue to use freewill to destroy. It is not God doing it. It is humanity choosing to devour one another. We can keep choosing to tear down others in an attempt to feel better about ourselves. We can continue to use our strengths to bully or manipulate others to overcome some wrong done to us. We can continue to choose to ridicule and abuse others…including people we have never met. We can continue to call people names, falsely accuse others, spread lies, and contribute to chaos, division, and hatred. We can even continue to justify the taking of someone's life because they do not agree with us.

This is **NOT** who God created Man or Woman to be. This is not God's heart for humanity.

God created a wondrous world and universe(s). The expanse of the stars on a clear night. The brilliance of sunrises and sunsets. The glories of each season as they flow from one into another. The budding of spring, the richness of summer, the glow of fall, and the quiet of winter. The amazement of the phases of the moon, the beauty of a full moon. What a sight to behold! A flower in bloom, the overwhelming fragrances of a bouquet. The sound and dance of wind as it moves through trees. And the animals, from the majestic elephant, to the uniqueness of a platypus, the roars of lions, the thundering hooves of horses, and the adoring eyes of a pet dog when you come home. All created by God!

A world designed for mankind to be blissfully and gloriously happy. An environment where mankind would have purpose, unity, and fulfillment. God created Man with incredible attributes perfectly designed to fulfill his destiny. God anointed Man with the ability to be a leader but not just a leader. God created him to be a strong, powerful leader, with passion and strength, embodied within his masculinity. God anointed Woman to be a strong leader, to be passionate, and to operate in wisdom. God also created Woman with incredible attributes perfectly designed to fulfill her destiny beautifully displayed within her femininity.

God created Man and Woman in His own image to be fruitful, multiply, fill the earth with goodness, subdue anything that was not in order with good, and to have dominion over the earth…not each other. He blessed man and woman to accomplish this purpose. His blessing still holds true.

When God finished, and He saw everything He had made, *"indeed, it was VERY GOOD."*

It is time to embrace and live in our God-given identities and gifts and fulfill God's mandate for our lives. We must start choosing to work together instead of working against each other. We need to build each other up rather than tear each other down. The time is now to stop competing against each other and come alongside one another to accomplish the greater good for all.

We can only do that when God is the center of our lives and He is our Source for all things. Time and time again humanity has tried to elevate themselves above God or remove God. Time and time again humanity has failed…and each time the cost consumed and destroyed lives.

Mankind, male and female, were created to live in the presence of God. Man and Woman are made in the image of God. Let us start living in the intrinsic worth God has created us all with. Let us choose to treat others in the wonder of the worth God created them in.

Man and Woman were created to live in the presence of each other as well. We were not created to diminish or destroy each other. God perfectly created us to come alongside Him and others to make this world a beautiful, wondrous, world.

There is beauty in Humanity.

Reflection

Chapter 5

1. Five chapters in, what new insights do you have regarding God's purpose for humanity to: *be fruitful, and multiply, and replenish the earth, and subdue it: and have dominion over it?*

_____
_____
_____
_____
_____

God created Man, *Ish*, **Aleph, Yod, Shin.**

2a. Write down characteristics of *Ish*:

_____
_____
_____
_____

2b. How does this impact your thoughts toward Man?

_____
_____
_____
_____

2c. What can you do to encourage these traits to develop in men?

_____
_____
_____
_____
_____
_____

God created Woman, *Ishah*, **Aleph, Shin, Hey.**

3a. Write down the characteristics of *Ishah*

_____
_____
_____
_____
_____
_____

3b. How does this impact your thoughts toward Woman?

_____
_____
_____
_____
_____
_____

3c. What can you do to encourage these traits to develop in women?

_____
_____
_____
_____
_____
_____

Ish and *Ishah* both contain **Aleph**: strong, power, leader, represented by the ox.

4. What does this say about both Man and Woman?

_____
_____
_____
_____
_____
_____
_____

We are to be yoked. We are yoked to God first.

5a. Where is God prioritized in the operation of your leadership qualities?

_____
_____
_____
_____
_____

5b. What happens when we, individually, are not yoked to God first?

_____
_____
_____
_____

We are to be yoked to others to achieve the like-minded vision we willingly come together to accomplish.

6a. What happens when we all want to be the lead ox, rather than willingly submitting to the yoke of where our strengths are best utilized?

_____
_____
_____

6b. What changes in your life do you need to make to become a student? (Remember, we can all learn.)

_____
_____
_____
_____

6c. What changes in your life do you need to make to become a better teacher?

_____
_____
_____
_____
_____

6d. What changes in your life do you need to make to become joyful in your strengths and recognize your contribution to the overall purpose is important, regardless of your position?

_____
_____
_____
_____
_____

Marriage is a unique type of yoke because it requires a different level of intimacy. But it is no different in its concept of being yoked together. Husband and Wife both carry **Aleph**.

7. How can **Aleph** be balanced in a marriage, so strife and division do not destroy the marriage?

_____
_____
_____
_____

Ish and *Ishah* both contain **Shin**: tooth or teeth, press, eat, two, representing carefully chewing over something; and it represents strength. It also represents the ability to remain strong regardless of the circumstance, and it represents the ability to change for the good.

8a. What does this say about both Man and Woman?

_____
_____
_____

8b. How is the ability to chew over something reflected in masculine characteristics?

_____
_____
_____
_____

8c. How is the ability to chew over something reflected in feminine characteristics?

_____
_____
_____
_____

8d. How can the potential differences in how **Shin** operates in Man and Woman bring value to the situation?

8e. How can the potential differences in how **Shin** operates in Man and Women bring division?

8f. What can you do to help prevent division when others are "chewing over something"?

Ish and *Ishah* both have the ability to remain strong regardless of the circumstance.

9a. How can this work in the favor of both?

9b. How can this work to the detriment of both?

Ish and *Ishah* both have the ability to change for the good.

10. How does this reconcile with the excuse, "I could not help myself" or "Well, it is just the way I am"?

_____
_____
_____
_____

Ish and *Ishah* both carry the general dimensions of a person: *emotions; intellect; will and pleasure.* And the nine impartations that come within those dimensions: *justice; mercy; kindness, understanding; application of knowledge; flash of an idea, severity or discipline; mercy or compassion; kindness.*

11a. What do these traits reveal about God?

_____
_____
_____
_____

11b. What do these traits reveal about the capabilities of Man and Woman?

_____
_____
_____

Ish, Man, contains, **Yod**: strength, hand, work, make, throw, worship (as in a Warrior). **Yod** represents holding something, synonymous with power or might, to fall in one's hands…implies a deed done, or a finished work.

12a. What does this reveal about God's desire for Man?

_____
_____
_____
_____
_____

12b. How does this reconcile with the notion that Man is owed something, rather than having to work for something?

_____
_____
_____
_____
_____

12c. How is God tying in Man's work as worship?

_____
_____
_____
_____
_____
_____

12d. How are God's traits to Man, strength, hand, work, make, throw, worship, reflective of Man as a Warrior?

_____
_____
_____
_____
_____
_____
_____
_____

Ishah, Woman, contains **Hey:** behold, reveal, breath, revelation, it is a representation of beholding something incredible, and being awestruck by its wonder. It is a portrayal of an open window providing a unique view.

13a. What does this reveal about God's desire for Woman?

_____
_____
_____
_____
_____

13b. What are some ways Woman operates in seeing things from a different perspective?

_____
_____
_____
_____

13c. What do you think happens to Woman's being when she loses her sense of wonder?

_____
_____
_____
_____

13d. How can Woman protect her ability to behold the world around her without diminishing the identity of others?

_____
_____
_____
_____

Ish, contains **Yod**, *Ishah* contains **Hey**, both contained in the Name of God, YHVH (Yahweh) *Yod, Hey, Vav, Hey*.

14a. What does this tell you about God's desire for relationship with Man and Woman?

_____
_____
_____
_____
_____

14b. What does this tell you about Man's and Woman's need for God?

_____
_____
_____
_____
_____

14c. How does this reflect the importance of Man's and Woman's connection with God?

Vav is the connecting hook that represents the connection between spiritual and earthly matters. It represents the connecting force of Almighty God that BINDS together heaven and earth.

15a. Given it is God who binds heaven and earth, how effective do you think mankind's efforts to sever the tie will ever be?

15b. What is the inevitable outcome when Mankind attempts to remove God from earth? Remember, God will not violate man's freewill, but He will respond to it.

When you remove *Yod* from Man and *Hey* from Woman, you are left with, *Aleph* and *Shin*, which means fire, a consuming fire.

16a. When you have fire, a focused, in control fire and directed by good motives, what does fire accomplish?

16b. When fire is unable to be controlled, contained, or is directed by evil intent, what does fire do?

16c. Who does this type of fire end up ultimately destroying?

Ish and *Ishah* both contain similar and unique traits.

17a. Does this mean that only Man operates in work/warrior strength and Woman cannot?

Why or why not?

17b. Does this mean that only Woman operates in wisdom and Man does not?

17c. Is there any indication that God created Man or Woman less than the other?

18. What do you think God's intent was creating *Ish* and *Ishah* similar, but different?

19. How can *Ish* and *Ishah* work together to CHANGE FOR THE GOOD without destroying one another in the process?

20. What are some thoughts regarding the truth that you are to live in the presence of God?

Other Revelations:

Chapter 6

Well, That Explains It!

Oh, Genesis 3, if we would only learn its lessons. There is an entity who hates God, and his sole purpose is to steal, kill, or destroy anything or anyone God holds dear. This, by the way, is everything associated with creation and humanity.

This entity, lucifer, satan, the devil, was by many studies, considered an archangel, alongside Michael and Gabriel. He thought quite highly of himself and believed it possible to surpass God. It is his desire to be worshipped. His arrogance and rebellion not only got him cast out of heaven but also those angels who chose to follow him in his rebellion. According to Revelation 12:4, one-third of the angels fell with satan…a heavy price to pay for choosing the wrong path to follow.

The enemy's tactics against humanity are still the same.

> *"Now the serpent was more subtil than any beast of the field which the Lord God had made."* (Genesis 3:1a, KJV)

Serpent, represents satan, its Hebrew translates literally to a snake, a serpent (Strong's 5175). Well, that is not too exciting. But when you dig a bit deeper, its root is found in 5172, which means, -*to hiss, a whisper.* It also references enchanter, enchantment, learn by experience, diligently observe. This becomes important to understand as satan has diligently observed mankind for a long time. He knows how to whisper into our vulnerabilities to influence us into choosing things that bring forth destruction.

Subtil, artfully, cunningly, craftily.

The serpent, an artfully, cunning, and crafty enemy of God hissed, whispered, into Woman's ear. This tactic is still being used to draw people away from God. The serpent started the conversation with a reasonable question:

> *"And he said to the woman, "Has God indeed said, 'You shall not eat of every tree of the garden'?"* (Genesis 3:1b)

First, she listened to a voice that contradicted God's voice.

Then, Woman adds a little bit more to the instructions of God. Man and Woman tend to do that. God never said they could not touch the tree or its fruit. He said do not eat of it.

> *"And the woman said to the serpent, "We may eat the fruit of the trees of the garden; but of the fruit of the tree which is in the midst of the garden, God has said, 'You shall not eat it, nor shall you touch it, lest you die.'"* (Genesis 3:2-3)

Here comes the subtle manipulation of the Woman and the Man.

> *"And the serpent said to the woman, "You will surely not die. For God knows that on the day that you eat thereof, your eyes will be opened, and you will be like angels, knowing good and evil."* (Genesis 3:4-5, The Complete Jewish Bible, with Rashi Commentary)

The King James Version says, *"ye will be as gods."*

In this whisper, the serpent caused doubt about God's Word and about death. He planted a seed that their eyes would be opened, and they would become like the angels or as a god. Humanity still struggles with the desire to be a god.

> *"And when the woman **saw** that the tree was **good for food**, and that it was **pleasant to the eyes**, and a **tree to be desired to make one wise**, she took of the fruit thereof, and did eat, and gave also unto **her husband with her**; and he did eat."* (Genesis 3:6, KJV, emphasis added)

The Woman then began to reason within herself to justify what the whisper had planted in her mind and opened her eyes to.

"good for food"

That sounds reasonable, yet God had given them every herb, and every tree for food...but they were enticed to eat from the only one He instructed them not to eat from.

"pleasant to the eyes"

It did not look like it would kill you. So, can it really be as bad as what my CREATOR said it would be?

*"a tree to be **desired** to make one **wise**"*

HEY! I am created to behold and to see things from a different perspective. I am supposed to be wise. Surely, by eating this fruit I will get smarter faster! Woman has a desire to become wise. And Mankind should desire wisdom, *that comes from the Lord.*

But this is not the Tree of Wisdom, it is the Tree of Knowledge of Good and Evil. The Woman mistook having your eyes opened to something that was never meant to be known as being wise…like God. It was not. There are somethings that God NEVER wanted humanity to have their eyes open to and see.

Knowledge of good and evil is not wisdom. Just because you have knowledge about something, does not mean you understand the right way to apply it. Wisdom guides you through the proper application of knowledge.

Desired, to delight in, greatly beloved, **covet,** delectable thing, delight, desire, goodly, **lust,** pleasant thing, precious thing (Strong's 2530, emphasis added).

Wise, make or act circumspect, and hence **intelligent, consider,** expert, instruct, **proper,** prudent, have **good success,** teach, **make to understand,** *wisdom, wise* (Strong's 7919, emphasis added).

The Woman desired to be made wise…problem was, she already had been created for great wisdom.

This is the Tree of Knowledge of Good and Evil that God planted in the Garden of Bliss. It is the one tree He commanded Man and Woman not to eat from. I have heard teachings that the Tree of Knowledge of Good and Evil was somewhere in the Garden. My studies, and my current revelation and understanding, have led me to believe that the Tree of Knowledge of Good and Evil was in plain sight of the Tree of Life. Both Genesis 2:9 and 3:3 refer to the Tree of Knowledge of Good and Evil as being in the midst, the middle, of the Garden. This, in my opinion, ties into the responsibility God places on every individual to choose…obedience or rebellion, life or death.

God is not intimated by Woman or Man having knowledge. After all, He gives Woman and Man knowledge in all areas of life, an example is given in Exodus 31:3. Knowledge can also a Spiritual Gift, a list is given in 1 Corinthians 12.

He, however, will not take second place to knowledge. The relationship with Life, the Source of Life, should always come before a relationship with knowledge. Life oversees the knowledge; knowledge should never dictate Life.

The Tree of Knowledge of Good and Evil, is not about having nor gaining knowledge. God created Mankind with a mind to reason, grow intellectually, have ideas, make decisions…to acquire information and learn. But the knowledge of good and evil positions Mankind to become its own moral compass. Mankind, not God, determines what is right and what is wrong. When Mankind determines what is right and wrong without God, a heavy price is paid. Look at history, when everyone does what is right in their own eyes, there is chaos, confusion, and great destruction.

Still to this day, Man and Woman presume we can use knowledge to replace or outsmart God. The enemy uses this tactic all the time. Knowledge did not replace nor outsmart God then, and it will not today. It did not remove the consequence of death then, and it will not remove the consequence of death today. The damage pursuing knowledge without God first…creates a fire that consumes and destroys. It is the manifestation of *Aleph* and *Shin*.

The harm that comes from using knowledge without godly wisdom is substantial and far reaching. It can even have generational damage.

> *"so she took of its fruit, and she ate, and she gave also to her husband with her, and he ate."* (Genesis 3:6b)

Both Man and Woman listened to the whisper of the serpent. They allowed themselves to be drawn away from the commands of God and their eyes were opened. And, consequences, life altering consequences followed…just as God had said.

Man and Woman forgot that they were created to keep and tend the Garden. They were given dominion over anything that was not in order with God's design. The serpent pointblank spoke against the instruction, the commands, of God. Right then and there, either one of them or both of them should have stopped the conversation and prevailed against it. The same rings true today. If something does not align with the Word of God, Man and Woman should rise and stand against it. Not by humiliating or devaluing a person, but stand against the knowledge, philosophy, that tries to exalt itself above God.

Man did not conduct himself in the manner God created him for. He did not look narrowly at the serpent and say, "Yeah, something is not right." Woman did not operate in her gifts and behold or chew on the situation and conclude that, "serpent, you are trying to trick me."

Neither the Man nor the Woman thought to even bring God into the situation. They knew the information contradicted what God said, which should have been their first clue to say no. But, even then, they could have chosen to go to God before they acted and discussed it with Him.

God had told Man and Woman to keep and tend, to subdue, and have dominion. This was His first instruction. They knew what the serpent was telling them did not align with God's Word. Therefore, their first reaction should have been, "No, you are out of order, you are trying to cause doubt, division, chaos and we will not have that in the Garden God has given us responsibility for. Now, get out!"

Before we start bashing Man and Woman, each of us should do an inventory of our own life. How many times have we heard a "whisper" that we knew did not "sit" right with us? We had this feeling something did not sound right? Yet, we talk ourselves out of those caution signs and proceed.

How many times do we hear a whisper we KNEW was not God? We KNEW it did not align with God's heart nor His Will, yet, we listened to it. We proceeded to come into agreement with it, rather than rejecting it. We got into a hot mess because of it, then blame someone else for it… even God. I am getting a little ahead of myself. I will talk more about that soon….

Man, nor Woman came to the aid of the other. Neither of them protected the other from listening to and ultimately agreeing to do something that was in direct opposition to God's command. This is more than one Man protecting one Woman. This goes to God's heart that humanity is supposed to protect humanity. The marriage commitment should be even more zealous to protect each other and the family unit.

> *"Then the eyes of both of them were opened, and they knew that they were naked; and they sewed fig leaves together and made themselves coverings."* (Genesis 3:7)

Their first response to, *"be as gods,"* was not joyous, excitement, or a new sense of power or strength. It was embarrassment. It was shame.

Shame, a PAINFUL sensation brought on by a consciousness of guilt, or of having done something which **injures reputation**; or by of that which nature or modesty ***prompts us to conceal***.

They tried to conceal what they had done by making inadequate coverings for themselves. They tried to fix the injury they had done. It did not work then, and it will not work today. Sin, rebellion against God's commands, still brings a sense of shame. No matter what people do to try and cover it up, even finding people that say it is okay. Sin always destroys something, no matter how big or how small we think the sin is.

Enter God.

> *"And they **heard** the sound of the Lord God walking in the garden **in the cool of the day**, and Adam and his wife **hid** themselves from the presence of the Lord God among the trees of the garden."* (Genesis 3:8, emphasis added)

The Man and the Woman both recognized the sound of the Lord God. That means God walking in the Garden to meet with them was a common event. Man and Woman BOTH hid themselves from the presence of God. How often do we do that as well? We make a mistake, we try to cover it up, but when that does not work, we try to HIDE.

We operate under the very misguided idea that if we can hide what we have done, then it will be okay. No one will be the wiser, no one will think ill of me, no one will get hurt. Nope. Hidden sin will destroy from the inside out. God knows this, and He is the only one who can redeem us from the sin. Yet, we still try to hide from Him.

The reality is, you, nor humanity, can hide from God.

> *"Then the Lord God called to Adam and said to him, "Where are you?"* (vs. 9)

God did not lose Adam. God called out to Adam to let Adam know where Adam was. He was revealing to Adam that Adam was not in his created, anointed position.

> *"So he said, "I heard Your voice in the garden, and I was afraid because I was naked; and I hid myself." (vs. 10)*
>
> *And He said, "Who told you that you were naked? Have you eaten from the tree of which I commanded you that you should not eat?" (vs. 11)*

Adam heard God's voice. Adam tried to remove himself from God's presence because he realized he was naked. He became afraid because he felt exposed, vulnerable in the presence of God. So, he made an ineffective attempt to hide from the holiness of God.

God asks a question He already knows the answer to. Adam, as the strong, powerful, full of strength leader God created him to be took full responsibility for his actions. Nope!

Adam blamed God and the Woman in one response. *"The **woman whom You gave to be with me**, she gave me of the tree, and I ate." (vs. 12)*

> *"And the Lord God said unto the woman, What is this that thou hast done? And the woman said, The serpent beguiled me, and I did eat." (vs. 13, KJV)*

God gave Woman the same opportunity when He asked what have YOU done? This is a direct question for her personal responsibility for her actions, no one else's. The Woman attempted to shift some of the responsibility to the serpent. God still held her responsible for her actions.

I want to unpack the word *'beguiled'* a little bit. Other versions are translated, *"...deceived me,"*. Yes, there was deception, the Woman was deceived by the whispers of the serpent. But, beguiled is a little bit more crafty, subtle, and strategic.

Beguiled, *nâshâ*, pronounced, *naw-shaw* to lead astray, mentally to delude or seduce (Strong's 5377).

Woman, the tactics to destroy women is still the same. We are emotional and intellectual beings. God created us this way, *Ishah*, **Aleph**, **Shin**, **Hey**. Therefore, that is where Women are attacked. Women are too smart for an obvious attack, so, the whispers attempt to seduce Woman through a twist in their emotions or way of thinking.

If the whisper were apparent in its lack of logic or reality, Woman could quickly and easily chew through it and not be deceived. But a subtle, crafty whisper, that speaks to something Woman wants or to an insecurity Woman has, Woman tends to take the bait and starts toying with the thought.

"Did God really say…?"

Therefore, it is so important to *personally* know what God says, and reveals, about Himself, about Man, and about Woman. Everything else is a distortion of the truth (which is a lie), and it is meant to destroy God's relationship with Man and Woman, destroy relationships between Man and Woman, and destroy Man and Woman individually.

When Man and Woman's eyes were opened, their response was an emotional response. They were so overwhelmed with the reality they found themselves in that they did not take a breath and operate in who God created them to be. I am taking latitude here to chew on this situation. Why? Because if humanity today would learn from the actions of others…and most importantly, what God did and is doing, then perhaps we would save ourselves and others from unnecessary pain.

"be as gods"

They already were created in the image and likeness of God. You, Man or Woman, are created in the image and likeness of God. We resemble and reflect God. So, quit trying to become someone you were not meant to be and focus on becoming who God fashioned you to be. Humanity, no matter how hard we try, cannot eliminate, destroy or become God.

"…shall not eat it, nor shall you touch it,"

God never said do not touch it, but Woman added to the command. Often, additions, restrictions, and quite frankly, ungodly addendums are given in the Name of God, even in the church, and, without asking God and chewing on them with the Word of God as their guide, humanity starts to abide by them…and they were NEVER of the Lord.

"…tree was good for food, pleasant to the eyes,"

There were possibly hundreds of thousands of trees and herbs available for food, but this one was the one thing Mankind was not supposed to eat. Mankind has gotten into so much trouble because when we are told we cannot or should not have something, it tends to make us want it more. Covetousness never ends well, neither does rebellion against God's commands.

Man and Woman kept staring at the one thing they should not have instead of staring at the abundance they did have…and it caused them great pain. They did not make the conscience decision to turn their eyes away from what they should not have been focused on.

"desirable to make one wise…"

There is a difference between wisdom and knowledge. Knowledge can be learned; true wisdom must be asked for. Woman was created with a great capacity for wisdom. The problem was, she pursued the wrong source to gain wisdom.

Humanity still does the same thing. Humanity pursues knowledge without gaining the wisdom to apply it appropriately. Great damage follows in the wake of unrestrained knowledge. Often taking years, even generations, to undo the damage.

Knowledge generated the ability to detect the miracle of a baby's heartbeat in the womb.

Knowledge also produced the ability to destroy it.

I enjoy the *Jurassic Park* movies. In the first movie, Jeff Goldblum's character, Dr. Ian Malcom makes this very profound statement about the difference between knowledge and wisdom:

> *"Your scientists were so preoccupied with whether or not they **COULD** that they didn't stop to think if they **SHOULD**."*

The desire of knowledge asks, "can we?" The desire of wisdom asks, "should we?"

"…and they knew that they were naked;"

They had been naked this entire time before the Lord. It did not seem to bother Him. Yet, when they realized that their disobedience resulted in exposure, they did not run to Him. They did not stop to think that they had been naked before Him all this time, and it was not an issue. They decided, out of shame and fear, to run from Him and feebly attempted to cover themselves up.

Mankind is still naked before the Lord. He knows our thoughts. He sees our actions. He looks at our hearts. Our clothing, our good deeds, our secrets, our feeble attempts to cover ourselves are ineffective. There is nothing hidden from the Lord. He. Sees. You. And He still loves you.

"they heard the sound of the Lord God…hid themselves from the presence of the Lord God,"

Both Man and Woman heard the sound of the Lord, they both knew it, they both were familiar with it. Every previous encounter, by all accounts in Scripture, had been joyous, exciting, blissful, and wondrous. Yet, they allowed shame and fear to overshadow what they already knew to be true. He was their Creator, and He had always shown Himself patient, kind, and gentle. Choose, in every circumstance, to run to Him, not away from Him.

"Where are you?"

The Lord is asking you right now, "Where are you?" God is the same yesterday, today and forevermore. He is still calling out to Man and Woman, where are you?

The challenge that Man and Woman faced in the Garden are the same challenges we face today. Their story explains the temptations we face and the struggle we go through. The choice remains to be beguiled by the whisper or trust God.

Chapter 6

Reflection

The devil is real. He is cunning, deceitful, and seeks to destroy humanity.

1. How seriously do you take the adversary that attempts to destroy you?
___
___
___
___
___
___
___

Why?
___
___
___
___
___
___

The enemy is portrayed as a serpent. When you trace this word to its root, it means: *-to hiss, a whisper*.

2. Why is this important to understand?
___
___
___
___
___
___

3. How does knowing that a tactic of the enemy is to whisper thoughts that cause doubt affect how you should respond to those whispers?

_____
_____
_____
_____
_____

Read Genesis 3:1-7 again.

4. What are some of the tactics the enemy uses to deceive?

_____
_____
_____
_____
_____

5. Why is knowing the tactics of the enemy important to know?

_____
_____
_____
_____
_____

6. Why do you think the Woman added to God's commands (vs. 2-3)?

_____
_____
_____
_____
_____

7. What impact does it have when you add to God's commands? Or when you blindly follow others who profess what God has commanded?

_____
_____
_____
_____

8. What did the adversary whisper that tempted the Woman and Man to disobey God?
_____
_____
_____
_____
_____

9. Was ALL that the adversary whispered a lie?
_____
_____
_____
_____
_____

10. Why do you think the adversary worked in this manner?
_____
_____
_____
_____
_____

11. List the three things the Woman reasoned with before she took the fruit and gave it to Man:
a) _____

b) _____

c) _____

12. How are those three things still used against Man and Woman today?
_____
_____
_____
_____
_____
_____

The Woman desired to be made wise. There is nothing wrong with desiring to become wise. But Woman made a critical error in learning to become wise.

13. What was she actually being enticed by?
___
___

14. Why was this the wrong way to go about gaining wisdom?
___
___
___
___
___
___

Knowledge is not a bad thing. Knowledge can empower, equip, and enable one to do incredible things. But knowledge must be processed through wisdom. A 3-year-old child should never have knowledge of violence, real or virtual. They do not have the mental capacity to wisely process what they are experiencing or seeing.

15. Write down your thoughts regarding the differences between knowledge and wisdom.
___
___
___
___
___
___

Think about your life.

16. Are there things that you wish you never had knowledge of? ___
What are they?
___
___
___
___
___

17. How did having that knowledge affect how you perceived yourself, others, or the world?

_____
_____
_____
_____
_____

Knowledge can easily become an idol, a type of belief system, that attempts to replace faith in God.

18. What are the dangers of pursuing knowledge without the instruction of God?

_____
_____
_____
_____
_____

Man and Woman's eyes were opened because they listened to whispers that were in direct conflict with God's command.

19. How is this relevant to you today?

_____
_____
_____
_____

20. What did Man and Woman forget when they started to listen to the whispers that drew them away from the instructions of the Lord God?

_____
_____
_____
_____
_____

21. What did Man and Woman forget to operate in when they began a conversation with "an entity" that caused them to question God's command?

___

22. Whose aid should Man or Woman have gone to when the "whisper" started to lure them into disobeying God?

___

23a. Does Scripture record that either the Man or Woman stopped and said, "We are going to ask God about this before we do anything?"

___

23b. Why do you think that was?

___

24. What should you do when you see or hear something that does not align with what God has said?

___

25. What was Man and Woman's first response when they disobeyed God's command?

26. What is your response when you do not listen to God?

27. What did Man and Woman do when they heard the presence of the Lord?

28. If God is anything like Creation and the Bible reveal Him to be, do you really believe that humanity can hide from God?

29. What does it do to you when you try to hide something you know is wrong?

God asked Man a yes or no question, *"Have you eaten from the tree of which I commanded you that you should not eat?"*

30. Why do you think Man's response was not a simple yes or no?

_____
_____
_____
_____
_____

31. Why do you think when confronted with misconduct we usually respond in the same manner, instead of a simple yes or no?

_____
_____
_____
_____
_____

God, just as He did the Man, directly asked the Woman about her personal actions.

32. What does this reveal about God and His relationship with people?

_____
_____
_____
_____
_____

Beguiled, to lead astray, mentally to delude or seduce. Man and Woman can still be beguiled.

33. Was it the Woman's eyes, heart, and/or mind that opened the door for the whisper to beguile her?

_____
_____
_____
_____
_____

34. How does this relate to us today?

35. What are some areas that Man is particularly susceptible to be deceived in?

36. What are some areas that Woman is particularly susceptible to be deceived in?

37. What are some safeguards that Man or Woman can put in place so they are not led astray, deluded, or seduced into destruction?

38. Why is it important to personally know what God has and has not said?

39. What are some of the lessons we can learn from the Man and Woman in Genesis 2?

40. What is your answer to God's question, *"Where are you?"*

Other Revelations:

Chapter 7

You Cannot Undo What You Have Done

Man, nor Woman, could undo what their decision had put into motion. God would not retract His warning that they would die if they disobeyed Him and ate from the one tree He told them not to. Their individual decision to participate in the disobedience led each of them to endure specific consequences.

God held each of them personally responsible for their choice. Again, this is a very important characteristic of God, individual action, individual responsibility, individual consequences. This does not mean that lives are not affected by the actions of others. It means each of us will endure the consequences of our actions, and we will be held personally responsible for them by God, whether people believe it or not.

The only being God cursed was the serpent. The ground became cursed because of the actions of Man. Man was supposed to dress and to keep the Garden. Instead, Man allowed disobedience into the Garden. When Man does not protect what God has given him responsibility over, destruction always follows.

God NEVER cursed Man or Woman!

God informed the serpent of the penalty and ultimate outcome of its part in the deception. It would be cursed more than every other animal; it would slither on its belly; and it would eat dust all the days of its life.

> *"Because you have done this, You are **cursed** more than all cattle, And more than every beast of the field; on your belly you shall go, And you shall eat dust all the days of your life.* (Genesis 3:14, emphasis added)

Cursed, **'ârar**, pronounced *aw-rar*, execrate (Strong's 779). The primary sense of execrate is to separate, literally to denounce evil against, to imprecate evil on; to detest utterly; to abhor; to abominate. I find the sense "to separate" interesting. I will leave that for another study.

God continues to inform the serpent of the status of the relationship between it and the Woman. And that through the Woman, the serpent would be brought to its eventual demise.

> *And I will put enmity between you and the woman, and between your seed and her Seed; He shall bruise your head, and you shall bruise His heel."* (Genesis 3:15)

Enmity, **êybâh**, pronounced *ay-baw*, hostility, hatred (Strong's 342) from the prim root **âyab**, pronounced, *aw-yab* to hate, as one of an opposite tribe or party, to be hostile—be an enemy (Strong's 340).

God put hatred, great hostility, between the enemy and Woman. Therefore, the battle to destroy Woman is intense. The enemy knows that for a Woman who has a relationship with God, she is an incredibly powerful opponent; they are from opposite tribes. Woman has within her the God-given attributes to discern, uncover, and overcome his work that destroys lives through his lies and deceit.

The enemy also knows that if he can influence Woman to his side, rebellion against God, then she can be used for great destruction. Remember, God created *Ishah* to be a strong leader, passionate, and to operate in wisdom. Woman's attributes were not revoked. Woman is still a strong leader and passionate and created with the capacity to behold situations from a different perspective. But when Woman chooses knowledge above God, destruction will be the end result. Woman, it is one or the other, no matter what other philosophies try to convince us of.

Reminder, God's original design included the possibility, the hope, of Mankind never having the knowledge of-evil, of shame, guilt, fear, or anything else that was not bliss. But, one choice that could not be undone, allowed this type of knowledge, this time of knowing, into the world. Pursing it set in motion consequences that only God can set right. Mankind can only choose to follow His plan or continue to rebel against Him.

The enemy also knew that through a Woman his demise would be brought forth. This is the first declaration of God's plan for Mankind to be redeemed…if they so choose. It is interesting that God speaks of seed regarding the Woman bringing redemption. Women do not carry the seed, Man does. Women carry the egg. The wonders of God.

God then told the Woman the consequences she would endure. Woman, you are not going to like the reality. But if you hold onto its Truth, then it will set you free from unfulfillment and a lot of destructive behaviors and choices. Who humanity was meant to be is found in Genesis chapters 1 and 2. It also reveals who we can be redeemed to become. With this understanding comes the clarity to remove distractions and whispers, and focus on what really matters: healing and restoration.

Every issue we face can be traced back to Genesis 3. Genesis 3:1-8 reveals humanity being tempted by the hiss, a whisper, to:
    1) rebel against God,
    2) attempt to become like a god,
    3) circumvent God's plan and process,
    4) not take our personal responsibilities seriously,
    4) justify our rebellious choices,
    5) choose what is desired through the distortion of coveting,
    6) not be grateful for what we have been given.

Thousands of years later, the battles remain the same. The same whispers hiss in our ears.

When we learn why and what battles we face, then we can overcome them and stop damaging ourselves, others, and the world. So, again, Woman, tap into your **Hey**, behold, get insight, and gain wisdom from a higher perspective.

Genesis 3:16 reveals why women deal with specific emotional responses that incorrectly frame situations women face. Women need to keep it in front of them because when you know why you are reacting a certain way; you can stop it before negative consequences follow an unwise response.

> *"Unto the woman he said, I will **greatly multiply thy sorrow** and thy conception; in **sorrow thou shalt bring forth children**; and thy desire shall be to thy husband, and he shall rule over thee." (KJV)*

"I will greatly multiply your sorrow…"

This implies that Woman could experience sorrow even before the rebellion. I found this interesting until I thought about the difference of experiencing sorrow with God verses without

Him. Sorrow spent in the presence of God still contains peace and comfort. Sorrow outside the presence of God bears despair, loneliness, hopelessness, bitterness, anger, and hatred.

God multiplied Woman's sorrow (herself), sorrow in conception (relationships), and sorrow in bringing forth children (raising children).

Sorrow, its-tsaw-boné, worrisomenesss, i.e. labor or pain—sorrow, toil, (Strong's 6093); from prim root, *aw-tsab´*, to carve, fabricate or fashion; hence (in a bad sense) to worry, pain or anger; displease, grieve, hurt, make, be sorry, vex, worship, wrest (Strong's 6087).

The first degree of Woman's sorrow is worry…just the very nature of worry. Women tend to worry about everything, even if the situation has nothing to do with them. Worry teases and harasses the mind and distorts clear thinking.

When I looked up worry in Webster's Dictionary 1828, two definitions caught my eye. Remember, that beholding attribute God gave Woman? I have learned when something keeps catching my eye, it is usually the Lord trying to reveal to me something more than surface meaning.

The first definition that caught my notices was: *"to fatigue; to harass with labor."*

Worry hinders Woman from beholding a situation from a place of peace and clarity, reducing her perspective to a place of fear and insecurity. This leads Woman to do what? Control.

Control causes Woman to become fatigued due to overworking trying to contain, manipulate, and determine an outcome she thinks should happen. The thought becomes if I work hard enough at this situation and FIX it, I will not need to worry. Control is exhausting, and control is an illusion. The only control humanity really has is the control of one's actions. Woman, nor Man, cannot control a situation or a person long-term. Sooner or later, the situation will fall apart, a person will resent you or rebel, and discouragement will overtake you. Then, the feelings of failure, fear, hopelessness, and despair will rear their ugly heads. These, if not subdued, will turn into a higher degree of manipulation and control — until the cycle takes on a life of its own, and you are held captive in its grip.

I am not saying Woman needs to pretend a situation is not happening and should not be addressed if it is out of God's order. Remember, Man and Woman were tasked with tending and keeping, putting things in order. But, when situations are approached without God and through the lens of worry, the outcome is not the best.

The second one, *"to harass by pursuit and barking; as dogs worry sheep."*

Dogs trained to watch sheep are an interesting thing. They are there to assist the shepherd with the sheep, normally doing no harm. But, if you have ever watched the sheep's response to the presence of the dog, it is an interesting lesson about worry. Picture a sheep dog sitting on the outskirts of the herd, just watching the sheep, and waiting for its next move. The sheep are doing sheep things, but they always have an awareness of the dog. He is constantly on their minds. As soon as that dog moves, the sheep tense up, maybe jump a little, or might even start to run. If one starts to run, they all start running…blindly and for no other reason than if one ran, surely, I should be running, too. They often scatter in chaotic directions until they are reigned back in… by the very thing that they started running from in the first place.

Worry is always there, in the back of Woman's mind, ready to leap to the forefront at the slightest inclination. Even if the "dog" simply moved to scratch a flea.

The sheep fabricated, fashioned, a scenario distorted by worry when there was never any real danger. Woman has been given by God the glorious ability to see things from multiple perspectives and then wisely decide the best course of action for all involved. Worry distorts this gift. Worry causes Woman to fabricate situations in her head when none of them actually exist.

God has given humanity the ability to deal with worry, and we will get to that in an upcoming chapter. But, if Woman and humanity, does not learn to properly deal with worry in the manner which God has given, the consequences continue to intensify.

Vex and *wrest* are two outcomes of unchecked worry. They are the product of the continual fabrication of situations viewed and born from worry.

Vex, to irritate; to make angry by little provocations, to torment, to disturb, to disquiet, to agitate.

Worry leads to anger. Worry's constant whisper in a Woman's mind can become a torment, disturbing a Woman's state of being causing an anger to rise and ultimately to lash out. Woman, vexed by the scenarios she has created in her mind, lashes out. The recipient, a child, a friend, a husband bears the brunt of anger due to an outcome fabricated in a Woman's mind.

Wrest, to twist or extort by violence; to take or force from by violence, to distort, to turn from truth or twist from its natural meaning by violence; to pervert.

Do you see the progression? There are a lot of violent actions caused by unrestrained, unsubstantiated, and unnecessary worry. Woman today have a violence within them that is being exhibited in brutal ways. Women lash out with vile, degrading, and vulgar words, rarely based on personal knowledge of the person or situation but based in hearsay.

Combined with a lack of knowing Woman's identity, physical violence by Women has escalated, and, in too many cases, eclipsed Man's. Women participate in horrific fights with other women. Women attacking men and expecting men not to defend themselves. Women beating, even killing, children in blind rages. Woman has escalated in the traits they have condemned Man for.

Too many women are becoming the very being Woman has been fighting against for centuries. Woman has fought to be treated as the equal God created her to be. Yet, instead of embracing the feminine strength and the beauty of her unique attributes, in the bondage of *wrest*, many women have allowed their words, behaviors, respect for self and others to deteriorate to levels far beneath the wonder that she is.

Worry, beloved Woman, manifests from feeling exposed and not feeling safe. So, Woman tries to cover herself and control situations in an attempt to feel secure.

But was it not God who multiplied Woman's sorrow, her worrisomenesss? Yes. Why?

Because God wanted and wants Woman to learn that it is only through a personal relationship with Him that she is covered, and she is secure.

Everything, and everyone else, including herself, any type of relationship or a husband, will always fall short because in ourselves, we are all insufficient. Without God in our lives, Woman desperately seeks protection, security, and companionship any way she can get it. This unfortunately is usually in unhealthy and increasingly emptier ways.

"In pain you shall bring forth children"

The word pain here is sorrow, but a little bit different than as defined above. It is from, *etseb*, pronounced, *eh-tseb*, which means an earthen vessel; usually painful toil; also, a pang (whether of body or mind); grievous, idol, labor, sorrow (Strong's 6089). Its prim root is the same as above. So, when left unredeemed, this pain will yield the same results as above.

Woman will worry and experience frustration about her children from conception until they are grown and leave the house…even after to some degree. Woman will painfully toil for her children, becoming a self-inflicted martyr, often resulting in the feeling of being unappreciated. Frustration enters, anger brews, lash out occurs…sounding familiar?

Woman in her sorrow, relinquishes her responsibility to tend, keep, and protect her children through busyness, pursuit of personal gratification, or to others. Woman has allowed society, including other women, to diminish the blessing of children and raising them well. There is NOTHING more purposeful and honorable than bringing forth children of integrity, intelligence, strong moral character, a heart to care for others, and the realization of the God who created them.

Because Woman's view of the miracle of birth and children has become distorted, more and more Women are justifying the exploitation and destruction of children. Woman, instead of protecting children, is exposing them to knowledge that they are NOT capable of processing wisely. This causes confusion in children's identity and purpose at an early age. Women are still listening to the whispers of *"your eyes will be opened"* to have knowledge of good and evil when it is not wise to do so.

God entrusted Woman to bring forth children. But without Him, Woman's pain to bring forth children only intensifies. Women are missing out on the true joy that comes from bringing forth children because women are listening to the whisper, that being a mom, particularly a stay-at-home-mom is causing her to miss out on…something.

A quick note of encouragement to those who are unable to bear children naturally. There are orphans in the world who need a Woman who will love them, protect them, and raise them. The Lord has a special place in His heart for the orphan. Adoption makes a man a father and a woman a mother just as deeply as biological procreation does.

There are also young people in this world desperate for a father and mother figure in their life. My biological father passed away a few years back. One of his students said this about him, *"He taught me how to fix a lawn mower, how to cut wood and build bird houses, cutting boards for my mom.* ***He taught the fundamentals the basics of how to become a man****. He taught me, and **I'm proof that a kid without a dad can succeed** thanks to his teacher!!!"*

For the Man and Woman who has chosen to end the life of a child through abortion: Abortion does not just go away once the abortion is done. The consequences of abortion are far-reaching and destructive. You can find healing and be set free from the guilt and shame from that decision. God has made a way.

This is the part of the verse that makes Women cringe. It is a difficult pill to swallow. It is misunderstood. It has been misapplied. And, it has been used to abuse and subjugate Woman to a value and role never intended by God. But it explains the tug-a-war between Husband and Wife and has now spilled out into relationships between Man and Woman. Too many Women, because of abandonment by fathers, disappointment and abuse by Man, have determined that the destruction of all Man will heal the pain. It will not.

> *"Your desire shall be for your husband, and he shall rule over you."*

"Your desire shall be for your husband,"

Desire, *tᵉshûwqâh*, pronounced, *tesh-oo-kaw,* stretching out after; a longing (Strong's 8669), from *shûwq*, pronounced, *shook*; a prim root **to run after or over**
(Strong's 7783, emphasis added).

Desire starts out as a hope, passion, a willingness to acquire and make her husband happy. But desire in this usage is a longing, beyond what is natural or normal, to control, overtake, or run over someone. It is a term that implies a trap to grab someone by the neck, throw them out of the way. It is the same term used in Genesis 4:7 when God was talking to Cain about why Cain's offering was not respected by Him.

> *"If you do well, will you not be accepted? And if you do not do well, sin lies at the door. And its desire is for you, but you should rule over it."*

God told Cain he could do better. But if he chose not to, then sin was ready to stretch out and grab hold of him. Sin was longing to overtake Cain, control him, and, if given free reign, destroy him. But God said Cain was to rule over the sin, to not let this happen. It is the same word "rule" used in both verses.

Cain did not control, rule over his sin, and he killed his younger brother, Abel. He became a fugitive and vagabond.

Woman, operating in *tesh-oo-kaw, shook*, stretches out after her husband, with an unnatural longing, to overtake him, control him, and destroy him. Her husband will take dominion over her and not let it happen.

If the Man is in right relationship with the Lord, and understands God's intent, then he will not rule over his wife at the expense of her value, identity, or purpose. He knows that God NEVER revoked *Ishah, Aleph, Shin, Hey*. Woman was still a partner to be fruitful, multiple, replenish the earth, subdue it, and have dominion over the creatures.

Right relationship is based on mutual respect and trust. There is a difference between knowing a religion and living based in relationship. A relationship with the Father transforms lives. Religion tends to operate in a controlling manner. There are many who have great knowledge of the Word of God, but they do not have the relationship with the Father, through Jesus Christ, to apply it to themselves and others with grace-filled wisdom. Please do not confuse, nor justify, being biblically counseled it is not wise to engage in behavior contrary to the Word of God as control.

If Man is not in right relationship with the Lord, then he will rule over his wife with harshness, neglect, abuse, apathy, and/or treat her as less than him. This, unfortunately, has occurred since God revealed the consequence of rebellion, producing an animosity toward marriage, the position of Husband, and has spilled into an overall rejection of Man.

Woman has made significant steps to overtake, control, even destroy Man. Woman, who should be nurturing boys to become, *Ish*, the wonder of *Aleph, Yod, Shin*, are conditioning them to deny their divine, God-given identities.

Remember, when you remove *Yod* from Man and *Hey* from Woman, you have destructive fire. Today, we see Man and Woman destroying themselves, Husbands and Wives destroying themselves (and their children in the process), and Man and Woman destroying each other. Fathers and mothers who profess to love their children are using them as pawns, or poisoning them against the other parent, to gain leverage in a divorce or to hurt the other parent. All this does is damage the children who need both a father and a mother to show them the fullness of *Ish* and *Ishah*, both individually and working together.

Humanity's continued effort to remove Father God from life will only bring more consuming and destructive fire. We are witnesses to destruction at every level and type of relationship, including Woman destroying Woman and Man destroying Man. The value of every human being is deteriorating in the eyes of humanity, allowing the destruction of any human for whatever reason, to be justified…by Mankind.

God NEVER intended one to dominate, rule over, another. And, even with the consequences Man and Woman set into motion, God still made a way for Man and Woman, Husband and Wife, to live as He created them to.

Man, too, was informed of his consequences. And, as with Woman, the repercussions of his disobedience explain a lot of what Man struggles with and experiences today.

> *"Cursed is the ground for your sake; In toil you shall eat of it all the days of your life. Both thorns and thistles it shall bring forth for you, and you shall eat the herb of the field. In the sweat of your face you shall eat bread till you return to the ground, for out of it you were taken; for dust you are, and to dust you shall return."* (Genesis 3:17b-19)

"Cursed is the ground for your sake;

The land that God created to bring forth grass, herbs, and trees was now cursed because of the actions of Man. The ground would no longer be a cooperative environment towards Man's efforts to tend and keep the Garden.

"In toil you shall eat of it all the days of your life."

Work shifted from a joyous, cooperative, and harmonious experience, to, yes, you got it, sorrow, worrisomeness (Strong's 6093). Tending and keeping the environment would become difficult, producing would only come forth through "daily grind." Work will become a constant nagging in the back of Man's mind. He would become consumed by it, and unfortunately, work, unredeemed, would become Man's identity. Through work, Man attempts to make a name for himself. Work would take priority over Man's relationship with God — wrong order, just like Woman choosing knowledge over relationship with God.

"Both thorns and thistles it shall bring forth for you, and you shall eat the herb of the field."

Thorns, qôwts, pronounced, *kotse,* in the sense of pricking, a thorn, from prim root, *qûwts,* pronounced, *koots,* to clip off; used only as a demon, to spend the harvest season; from *qayits,* pronounced, *kah-́yits,* harvest (as the crop), whether the products, grain or fruits
(Strong's 6975, 6972, 7019).

Man will sweat in his labor and for his efforts, the environment will produce things that will incessantly cause Man to worry. The harvest season will be done with a sense of constant pricking.

Prick, to pierce with a sharp instrument or substance; to affect with sharp pain.

Ouch.

Thorns represent worldly cares and things which prevent the growth of good principles. Man will become so consumed by work, and by becoming successful through work, that work enslaves Man. Work begins to control Man rather than Man controlling (subduing) work.

Work, *to tend and keep*, was meant to be done in relationship with God, not against Him and certainly not without Him. When Man chooses work as his identity and value, work ceases to be an act of worship, and it becomes an idol. The idol of work becomes an addiction. When work addiction loses the initial satisfaction gained from accolades, it opens the door for other addictions.

These addictions run the gamut from excessive exercise and obsessive sports to alcoholism and pornography, to name a few. Addictions are anything that masks the pain and emptiness in a void that only a relationship with God can fill.

Thistles, dardar, pronounced, *dar-dar,* means thistle, thorn (Strong's 1863). There is no meaning wasted in the Word of God, so thistle represents more than another thorn, which was already mentioned. When we see something that seems repetitive, it is best to seek out the matter. Webster's Dictionary 1828 gives some interesting knowledge to go deeper into what God was communicating to Man.

Remember, God created Man to tend the Garden. So, with that reference in mind, how does thistle fit with thorn and the consequences Man set in motion?

Thistle, the common name of numerous prickly plants of the class Syngenesia, one species of thistle (Cnicus arvensis) grows in fields among grain and is extremely troublesome to farmers.

And there it is: *grows in fields among grain and is **extremely troublesome to farmers.***

The environment will be troublesome to Man. It will be a constant disturbance, annoyance, and vexing to Man all the days of his life. It will become burdensome, tiresome, and wearisome. And, if the Man, or the ground, remains unredeemed, they are both destroyed.

Women, who take Man's position as it relates work, are subjected to these same consequences. Work has become too many Women's identity and value. It will have the same effect as it has had on Man, burdensome, tiresome, and wearisome. And, if left unredeemed, will destroy. Destruction is the nature of things that are not in proper order.

*"In the **sweat** of your face you shall eat bread till you return to the ground,"*

Sweat, zêâh, pronounced, *zay-aw,* from 2111 (in the sense of 3154); perspiration, sweat (Strong's 2188).

Zûwâ, pronounced, *zoo-ah*, a prim root; to shake off, to agitate (as with fear): move, tremble, vex (Strong's 2111).

In the sense of, *yeza,* pronounced, *yeh-zah,* from an unused root mean to ooze; sweat; by implication, a sweating dress (Strong's 3154).

There is so much more in this seemingly obvious word. Man will bring forth sustenance through the sweat of labor. Man will sweat in his labors so much, he will have to shake off the droplets. Agitation is brought on by the fear of not being able to provide. Man's inner being trembles, he is vexed and tormented by the idea that he and his labor are not enough. He will ooze sweat all the days of his life.

Interesting note, God considers sweating unholy or unclean. He instructed the priests, "not bind themselves with anything that causes sweat." (Ezekiel 44:17, 18) Sweat came in with sin; it was not a part of God's design that Man sweated in the agitation of fear. Sweat today is such an issue, there is clothing made specifically for those who sweat too much. There is even a medical condition for excessive sweating.

Face, aph, pronounced, *af,* the nose or nostril, hence the face, occasionally a person: also (from the rapid breathing in passion) ire:-anger (angry) (Strong's 639), from *ânaph,* pronounced, *aw-naf,* prim root, to breathe hard, to be enraged; - be angry, displeased (Strong's 599).

There is a lot of anger produced when you work and work and work and nothing seems to happen as one desires. Man comes home from a particularly difficult thorn and thistle day; anger is simmering below the surface. In an attempt to control himself or deal with the day, Man grabs a beer, sits in front of television set, ignores the family, and disengages from life. Woman, vexed by worry, tries to engage with Man, Man explodes… Are you starting to see the root of so many of life's situations? If left unredeemed, Man and Woman continue to move towards destruction, then and now.

"till you return to the ground, for out of it you were taken; for dust you are, and to dust you shall return."

This is a harsh, but necessary, reminder, that humanity is not, and will never become, God. Humanity has tried for centuries to exalt themselves as a god. It has never ended well, and any attempt has been at the great expense of others.

Humanity, Man and Woman, are created in the image according to the likeness of God. We are from but are not only dust. We have the breath of God breathed into us. Arrogance has no place because we are but dust. Unworthiness has no place because we are made in His image. It is a delicate balance of confidence that comes from security and humility that comes from connectedness.

> *"Also for Adam and his wife the Lord God made tunics of skin, and clothed them."* (Genesis 3:21)

Adam and Eve attempted to cover their nakedness; it was not sufficient. God, in His mercy, provided covering for them that covered their nakedness, provided modesty, and elevated them above animals. Animals had no fear of Man until after the flood receded in Genesis 9:1-3. A fear and dread of Mankind fell upon the animal world.

> *"Then the Lord God said, "Behold, the man has become like one of Us, to know good and evil. And now, lest he put out his hand and take also of the tree of life, and eat, and live forever" therefore the Lord God sent him out of the garden of Eden to till the ground from which he was taken. So He drove out the man; and He placed cherubim at the east of the garden of Eden, and a flaming sword which turned every way, to guard the way to the tree of life."* (Genesis 3:22-24)

God removed Man and Woman from the Garden because He did not want them to live forever setting their own moral code of good and evil. The standard of what is good and what is evil is set by God and God alone.

Genghis Khan, Idi Amin Dada, Vlad III, Pol Pot, Kim II Sung, Saddam Hussein, Adolf Hitler, all set their standard, their own moral code. What was the cost? Mao Tse-Tung set his standard, and it is estimate he is responsible for as many as 49,000,000 lives. Vladimir Lenin and Joseph Stalin set their moral code. It is estimated upwards of 26,000,000 died. Can you imagine the cost if they, and others like them, lived forever?

Women do not think, "Well, that figures, those are Men. Aileen Wuornos, Kate Bender, Judias Buenoano, Bella Gunness, Juana Barraza, Diane Downs, Jane Toppan, Gesche Gottfried, Amelia Dyer, Kristen Gilbert, Megan Huntsman, Dorothea Puente and Nannie Doss all set their personal moral code. They committed some of the most horrific acts imaginable.

Well, you might be thinking, something extreme must have caused them to do such horrific acts. We currently live in a culture where people justify killing someone because they have different political views. People can steal, destroy businesses, and vandalize homes all under the pretense of protest, victim mentality, and entitlement. Someone can come into your home, harm your family, rob you blind, stub their toe and press charges against you. Humanity cannot set the standard of what is good and what is evil. Humanity certainly cannot administer any type of justice without the wisdom of God.

God gave Mankind The Ten Commandments to reveal and teach humanity what is good and evil, right and wrong. The Ten Commandments are our moral compass.

Genesis 1 and 2 reveal God's original design of creation, Man and Woman…and it was good, very good. God created Man and Woman in His likeness to reveal His attributes.

God created Man and Woman to be in direct, face-to-face, relationship with Him.

God blessed the Man and Woman to fulfill their assignment. Man and Woman were created to work together, to utilize their unique characteristics to carry out their God-given purpose to tend, keep, and subdue the earth in all its beauty and wonder.

God created them equal but different, and neither were meant to rule over the other.

Disobedience opened the door to shame, trembling fear of and separation from God, and brought forth sorrow, sweat, and discord. It opened the door for the destruction of Man and Woman by Man and Woman.

Thousands of years later, we still battle with the same deceptive whispers Man and Woman faced in the Garden. We also continue to battle with the consequence's disobedience caused and causes.

God gave us an account of creation so that we would have revelation of Him and His intention for Man and Woman. Revelation becomes understanding; we begin to understand, to comprehend how things truly work, or should work according to God. We get on God's page. Understanding produces knowledge, which brings clarity of that which exists, it is of truth and fact…not opinion, theory, or philosophy.

Revelation, understanding, knowledge processed with God, and through HIS moral code, produces wisdom. Wisdom is required to apply revelation, understanding, and knowledge accurately, suitably, gracefully, and humbly for the betterment of humanity.

Without God, all is tainted and will end in destructive fire.

We cannot undo decisions we have made in the past. But God, through His mercy, established the path to redemption. God, as He did in the Garden, presented humanity with a choice. Choose Life or choose death.

The decision is yours.

Chapter 7

Reflection

Once decision have been made, and action has been taken, you cannot undo what has been done.

1. How does this put into perspective the importance of thinking about the decisions you make?
___
___
___
___
___

We must make decisions and take action to accomplish things. So, we cannot be indecisive, or paralyzed by fear of making a mistake or of failure.

2. What, then, do we need as foundational information from which all decisions are based?
___
___
___
___
___

3a. Who is the only being cursed by God?
___
___
___
___

3b. Why is this important to understand and what does it reveal about God?
___
___
___
___

God informs the serpent and the Woman what their relationship would entail…enmity, an intense hatred.

4a. How does this explain some of the animosity towards Woman?

_____
_____
_____
_____
_____
_____
_____
_____
_____

4b. How should this focus Woman on who she is fighting?

_____
_____
_____
_____
_____
_____
_____
_____
_____

God said, *"between your seed and her Seed; He shall bruise your head, and you shall bruise His heel."*
God is referring to the redemption of Mankind through Jesus Christ.

5. What does this reveal about God's hope towards Mankind by establishing the path to redemption when Mankind disobeyed His command?

_____
_____
_____
_____
_____
_____
_____

God informed Woman of the consequences Women would endure because of disobedience. Woman's sorrow is greatly multiplied, in herself, conception and bringing forth children. Sorrow is reflected in worrisomenesss.

6a. What does *"to fatigue; to harass with labor"*, *"to harass by pursuit and barking; as dogs worry sheep,"* mean to you?

_____
_____
_____
_____
_____
_____
_____
_____

6b. How is worry reflected in your life?

_____
_____
_____
_____
_____

6c. How much "control" do you try to exert in your life, in others' lives, and in situations in an attempt to manage worry?

_____
_____
_____
_____
_____
_____

7. How does worry distort how Woman views herself and life around her?

_____
_____
_____
_____
_____
_____

We can become so accustomed to worry that it becomes suppressed in our subconscious. Then, when worry is not dealt with in healthy ways, worry produces *vexing* (irritation) and *wresting* (to twist or extort by violence) in people's lives.

8a. What evidence do we see that worry has escalated to vexing and wresting in Woman and Man?

_____
_____
_____
_____
_____
_____

8b. How does identifying the source of worry help Woman and Man to deal with worry in a healthy way?

_____
_____
_____
_____
_____
_____

"In pain you shall bring forth children" From conception to the child leaving the house, Woman will experience frustration.

9a. Why did God multiply sorrow in Woman?

_____
_____
_____
_____
_____
_____

9b. Does this mean God thinks less of Woman?

_____
_____
_____

9c. How does this reveal the foundational challenges and the struggles Woman wrestles with regarding bringing forth and personally raising her children?

_____
_____
_____
_____
_____
_____
_____

9d. How can Woman learn to overcome the sorrow regarding bringing forth children and embrace the blessing of children?

_____
_____
_____
_____
_____
_____

Woman faced additional challenges in her relationship with her husband, that has overflowed into her relationship with Man.

"Your desire shall be for your husband, and he shall rule over you."

This type of desire is not a healthy desire for the RIGHT things, but a desire that has been twisted. Women can wrestle with the desire to gain a husband…or now-a-days pursue a relationship. Then, in marriage or in a relationship, Woman can battle with an unhealthy desire (thoughts) to wring the Man's neck and take his place.

10a. Do you wrestle, beyond what is normal from living with someone 24/7, with wanting to wring your husband's neck and take his place?

_____
_____
_____
_____
_____
_____
_____

10b. How often do your words or actions degrade, devalue or de-humanize Man?

10c. How strong is the desire to take Man's place in:
A marriage:

The workplace:

In leadership positions:

In bringing up young boys to become more like Woman, *Ishah*, rather than Man *Ish*:

10d. Why is this important to recognize?

10e. Who, specifically, rules over whom?

10f. Does this consequence say anything about Man ruling over Woman?

10g. What specifically is God referring to regarding the Husband ruling over his Wife? Is it over her as a Woman/Wife, or is it over her actions when she attempts to *"take him by the neck, throw him away, and take his place"*?

11a. Given God did not revoke Woman's attributes and with her being a "different side to the same coin," how should a Husband "rule" over his Wife?

11b. What are some of the outcomes of a Husband ruling in an ungodly manner over his Wife?

12. What happens to Man and Woman when God is removed?

13. Did God ever intend for Man or Woman to rule over one another?

14. Who is the only Being meant to "rule" over them?

The ground became cursed because of Man's rebellion.

15a. How does this relate to Man's environment today?

15b. What shifted in Man's ability to produce sustenance for him and his family?

15c. What shift took place in Man's relationship with God and work?

15d. How has this affected Man and his identity?

_____
_____
_____
_____
_____
_____
_____

15e. What are the *thorns* and *thistles* that the ground would produce in Man's efforts of work?

_____
_____
_____
_____
_____
_____
_____

19. What is the long-term effect on Man's being (spiritually, emotionally, mentally, and physically)?

_____
_____
_____
_____
_____
_____

20. When Woman tries to take a Man's position by "becoming like a man", what is she opening herself to?

_____
_____
_____
_____
_____
_____

"In the sweat of your face you shall eat bread till you return to the ground,"

Man will produce through agitation, fear, trembling, constant, nagging sweat, resulting in an underlying anger that manifests in many ways.

21a. What is evidence of this consequence in Man's actions today?
___
___
___
___
___

21b. What toil has it taken on the identities of Man?
___
___
___
___

21c. How has it impacted the relationship between God and Man?
___
___
___
___

21d. Between Husband and Wife?
___
___
___
___

21e. Between Man and Woman?
___
___

22. Why do you think Man and Woman still attempt to become god(s)?
___
___

23. What are some ways Man and Woman attempt to become god-like?

24. Will Man or Woman ever succeed in their quest to become god(s)?

Why or why not?

25. What are the consequences to others when a Man or a Woman attempts to exalt themselves above others like a god?

26. Why was it insufficient for Man and Woman to attempt to cover themselves?

27. Do believe there is sin?
_____
_____
_____
_____
_____

Why or why not?
_____
_____
_____
_____
_____

28. Why do you think Man and Woman still attempt to cover their sins?
_____
_____
_____
_____
_____

29. How do Man and Woman still attempt to cover their sins?
_____
_____
_____
_____
_____

30. What happens when sin is not properly dealt with in your or someone else's life?
_____
_____
_____
_____
_____

31. Why did God remove Man and Woman from the Garden?

32. Do you believe that Man and Woman are capable of setting their own personal moral code?

Why or why not?

33. What are some consequences when Man or Woman sets moral codes?

34. How do you reconcile one's personal moral code when it conflicts with someone else's moral code?

35. Who gets to decide which moral code is the right one to follow and is fair for all?

36. Who must set the moral code for humanity?

37. Why does this prove out to be true?

38. What have you learned about God thus far?

39. What have you learned about Man?

40. What have you learned about Woman?

41. What have you learned about consequences to decisions?

42. What new knowledge have you received regarding any part of our journey together thus far?

Chapter 8

Redemption

You may be struggling with the idea of God or struggling with why He does what He does. That is okay. The God I believe in is big enough to handle your struggle…just struggle to Him, not against Him. This chapter may be difficult if the concept of needing a Redeemer is unknown to you, you have been ill-informed or misled, or you have been deeply wounded by someone who professed to be a follower of Jesus Christ, but their actions told a different story. I encourage you to continue this journey. Do not let incorrect or negative actions of others deter you from beholding your true identity, living in purpose, and abiding in peace.

Do not allow others to hinder your discovery of the One true Living God, who loves you deeply.

Humanity has fought it for centuries, but the Truth remains. We were created to be in right relationship with our Creator. True life only comes from living in the commands of God, pursuing the way of life He set the standard for. It is not easy, but it is obtainable. Because God made a way and always makes a way back to Him.

God never wanted humanity to have the knowledge of good and evil. He certainly did not want Man to live forever in that state. Cain, the son of Adam and Eve, murdered his brother. Cain was the next generation. Can you imagine if no one died by the aging process? The chaos history reveals is nothing compared to the chaos caused by people living forever.

> *"Then the Lord God said, "Behold, the man has become like one of Us, to know good and evil. And now, lest he put out his hand and take also of the tree of life, and eat, and live forever"—therefore the Lord God sent him out of the garden of Eden to till the ground from which he was taken. So He drove out the man; and He placed cherubim at the east of the garden of Eden, and a flaming sword which turned every way, to guard the way to the tree of life." (Genesis 3:22-24)*

God removed Man and Woman from the Garden of Bliss into a hostile environment where Man would till the ground and Woman would experience multiplied sorrows. God then placed a flaming sword to protect the road that led to the Tree of Life.

Just a little nugget to chew on –the Garden of Bliss is still there. God never said it was destroyed. It is simply hidden from our current sight.

God, at the rebellion of humanity, set in motion His plan for the redemption of the earth, which He said was *"good"*, and humanity, which He said was *"very good"*. I hope that makes you smile, God said you are *very good*…it is just sometimes we do not do very good things, and He needs to help us get back to wholeness.

Redeem, to purchase back; to ransom; to liberate or **rescue from captivity or bondage**, or from any obligation or liability to suffer or to be forfeited, by **paying an equivalent**.

The entire Old Testament is the implementation and unfolding of His plan to redeem. The Old Testament reveals God working out His plan through the decisions of humanity. It reveals God continually teaching humanity the consequences of living by standards fabricated through the idols of self-worship verses living by His standards. The Old Testament reveals a cycle of the degradation of humanity due to rebellion against God and God's continual restoration by Him… which was and continues to be, contingent upon the choices of Mankind.

Through it all, He set apart a remnant to keep His redemptive plan unfolding until its unveiling in Jesus Christ coming to earth. God sent Jesus Christ to earth to redeem humanity from their rebellion against God. It is through the birth, life, death at the Cross, and His resurrection that the road leading to Life is revealed.

Jesus Christ was there in the beginning of Creation. He was there at the creation of Man, when God breathed the breath of Life into humanity. He was there when humanity tried to hide from God. And, He was there when God revealed His plan of restoration…and revealed what it would cost God and Jesus Christ to redeem humanity.

Jesus is the Seed that God established at the rebellion, *"I will put enmity between you and the woman, and between your seed and her Seed; He shall bruise your head, And you shall bruise His heel."* (Genesis 3:15)

In the Garden, God gave humanity one requirement, do not eat from the Tree of Knowledge of Good and Evil. To be redeemed from the consequence of the rebellion, God has given one requirement, believe in My Son.

> *"Jesus said to him, "I am the way, the truth, and the life. No one comes to the Father except through Me."* (John 14:6)

Jesus Christ reveals the Father. He was and is a living example of the heart of God.

> ***"If you had known Me, you would have known My Father also;*** *and from now on you know Him and have seen Him.... Do you not believe that **I am in the Father, and the Father in Me?***
>
> *The words that I speak to you I do not speak on My own authority;* **but the Father who dwells in Me** *does the works. Believe Me that **I am in the Father and the Father in Me**, or else believe Me for the sake of the works themselves."*
> (John 14:7, 10-11, emphasis added)

God is the God of restoration. It is His heart. But He will not negate what He has established. He bestowed the gift of the freewill upon every person to choose…and with those choices, the responsibility to live with the consequences. Humanity might try to get out of personal responsibility, but God knows.

Restore, **to bring back or recover** from lapse, degeneracy, declension or ruin **to its former state.**

God's intent of restoration is to bring humanity back from a continual decline towards a worse state and to restore the desire to never settle for less than excellence…His excellence.

John 20 unveils such beautiful understanding of God's heart toward Woman. He boldly proclaimed for all to see that Woman is precious to Him. He boldly portrayed: I have redeemed her; I have restored her; I have revealed to her the beauty that is Woman.

Jesus had been crucified and laid in a tomb. Mary Magdalene went to the tomb and found the stone had been rolled away. She ran to Peter and John and told them, they ran to the tomb, and found it only contained the handkerchief folded separately, away from the linen cloths that wrapped Jesus' body. Remember, nothing is wasted in God's Word. I will let you seek out the significance of the handkerchief, folded and separated from the rest.

But they did not see what Mary sees. It was not revealed to Man, it was revealed to Woman.

Peter and John left, but Mary stood by the tomb, weeping. She was travailing within herself. This is an important note as we continue in our journey of who God has called Woman to be.
Then, she saw an amazing sight:

> *"And she saw two angels in white sitting, one at the head and the other at the feet, where the body of Jesus had lain."* (John 20:12)

This is important as it represents the manifestation of the Ark of the Testimony (Ark of the Covenant) of the Old Testament brought to life in Jesus Christ the New Testament Covenant of Grace. The Ark of the Covenant represented the presence of God to the people of Israel. It held the Ten Commandments, a bowl of manna, and Aaron's staff that budded. On its lid were two angels, facing each other with their wings covering their faces and a bowl was set between them. That bowl represented mercy. It also represented where God met with Moses (Exodus 25:17-22).

> *"You shall put the **mercy seat** on top of the ark, and in the ark you shall put the Testimony that I will give you. And **there I will meet with you**, and I will speak with you from above the mercy seat, from between the two cherubim,"* (Exodus 25:21-22a, emphasis added)

The angels asked Mary why she was weeping, and she told them that her Lord had been taken away. She then turned around and saw a man.

> *"Now when she had said this, she turned around and saw Jesus standing there, **and did not know that it was Jesus**. Jesus said to her, "Woman, why are you weeping? Whom are you seeking?" She, **supposing Him to be the gardener**, said to Him, "Sir, if You have carried Him away, tell me where You have laid Him, and I will take Him away."* (John 20:14-15, emphasis added)

She saw Jesus, talked with Him, but did not recognize who He was. Then, look at this, she thought He was the GARDENER! Sound familiar? A gardener, one who *tends* and *keeps*. God restored what was lost in a Garden, in a garden. Simply wondrous!

Let us behold another wonder of God's redemption. In the Garden of Eden, God brought Woman to be named by the Man. Once Man named her, she was released into her Womanhood and all the beauty God had imparted within her. Mary had turned her back on the gardener and started to walk away.

> *"Jesus said to her, "**Mary!**" She **turned** and said to Him, "Rabboni!" (which is to say, Teacher)."* (John 20:16, emphasis added)

When Mary was called by her name, her heart was opened, she turned back around and saw… her Redeemer, Jesus Christ was revealed to her. Behold, it was not Woman being presented to Man again. It was Jesus Christ presenting Himself to Woman, to heal her heart, open her eyes to redeem and restore her to her original identity and position.

Jesus is calling your name.

Jesus then says an interesting thing:

> *"Jesus said to her, "Do not cling to Me, for I have not yet ascended to My Father;"* (John 20:17a)

Why would Jesus stop Mary from hugging Him? Sounds a little rude and not very loving. But it reveals the importance of God redeeming Woman.

Jesus said, *"I have not yet ascended to My Father."*

God interrupted the resurrection process to reveal Jesus, the Redeemer, to Woman. He not only interrupted a very important redemption process; He also gave Woman an assignment.

> *"...**but go to My brethren and say to them**, 'I am ascending to My Father and your Father, and to My God and your God."* (John 20:17b)

What is Mary being told to do? Share the news! Let me put it in these words:

*"Be **fruitful**! Go and tell the brethren I am alive. **Multiply** the Good News that I am ascending to My Father and your Father; **fill** the earth and **subdue** it with the Truth that I go to My God and your God; have **dominion** over creation for I have <u>**redeemed**</u> it."*

Jesus Christ was revealed to a Woman first. This does not make Woman more important, valued, or loved than Man. It is God's bold statement of the fulfillment of Genesis 3:15:

> *"God told the serpent: "Because you've done this, you're cursed, cursed beyond all cattle and wild animals, Cursed to slink on your belly and eat dirt all your life. **I'm***

declaring war between you and the Woman, between your offspring and hers. He'll wound your head, you'll wound his heel."
(vs. 14-15, THE MESSAGE, emphasis added)

God reset creation and humanity back to His original design through Jesus Christ. Through Jesus Christ, not without Him, around Him, or despite Him, but with Him and through Him.

Jesus revealed Himself a little different to Man after His resurrection. There are several stories on how Jesus continued to reveal Himself to others. I would like to show how Jesus restored Man, specifically Peter. Peter, warrior, bold, confident, and passionate, and he loved Jesus deeply. He was also arrogant, hard-headed, and often fired before he aimed.

Peter fervently argued with Jesus he would not deny that he knew Jesus Christ, even if it cost him his life. (Luke 22:33-34) Peter does deny Jesus, just as Jesus said he would, and Peter is heartbroken. (Luke 22:54-62)

In Mark 16:4-7, an angel of the Lord tells the women to tell the disciples…*and Peter*, to go to Galilee. Peter is mentioned by name.

So, the Lord entrusted a Woman with a very important purpose. The same gender that listened to the whisper and chose to disobey Him in the Garden of Bliss. Imagine if the women who desired to follow Christ had continued to operate under any shame, guilt, sorrow, or listened to the whispers of society norms, cultural taboos, or whatever bondage may have held them back from listening to God. Behold the completeness of God's restoration!

In John 21, Jesus is on the shore and the disciples are out fishing, without much success. Jesus, whom they did not recognize, tells them to cast their nets on the right side of the boat. I find it interesting they had spent at least three years with Jesus, yet they did not recognize Him. They listened to the right voice, caught an abundance of fish, and something flickered inside them. John said it was Jesus, and Peter jumped into the sea to get to the shore.

Peter's response was to jump into the sea get to the shore. He did not allow the shame, guilt, sorrow or the whispers of any other voice to impede him. He listened to the voice of Jesus Christ. Jesus called Peter by name.

After they had eaten breakfast, Jesus turns to Peter and asks him three times if he loved Him. By the third time, Peter was grieved, sorrowful, heavy in his heart because Jesus asked him three

times. This was not to be cruel to Peter; Jesus knew Peter's personality. Jesus knew that by asking Peter three times if he loved Him, he would tend Jesus' sheep (people). Jesus "placed" Peter into his position and his purpose, to tend and to keep, so it would never be shaken again. Peter fulfilled what God, through Jesus Christ, had called him to do.
God redeemed Creation through Jesus Christ. God gave Man and Woman the opportunity to be redeemed and restored through Jesus Christ.

> *"And the gift is not like that which came through the one who sinned. For the judgment which came from one offense resulted in condemnation, but the free gift which came from many offenses resulted in justification. For if by the one man's offense death reigned through the one, much more those who receive abundance of grace and of the gift of righteousness will reign in life through the One, Jesus Christ.*
>
> *Therefore, as through one man's offense judgment came to all men, resulting in condemnation, even so* **through one Man's righteous act the free gift came to all men**, *resulting in justification of life."* (Romans 5:16-18, emphasis added)

Through Man (Adam), judgment and condemnation entered the world. Through Jesus Christ, grace and justification of life entered the world.

In John 20:21-23, an interesting event happens before Jesus Christ ascends to the Father:

> *"So Jesus said to them again, "Peace to you! As the Father has sent Me, I also send you." And when He had said this,* **He breathed on them,** *and said to them,* **"Receive the Holy Spirit.** *If you forgive the sins of any, they are forgiven them; if you retain the sins of any, they are retained."* (emphasis added)

When you trace back the Greek word, *ĕmphusaō*, pronounced, *em-poo-sah-o*, it means *"breathed,"* it also leads you to some very interesting depths.

It is first defined as, *to puff, to blow at or on* (Strong's 1720). Strong's takes you to, *en,* which is a prim root **denoting fixed position** *(in place, time or state)*, (Strong's 1722).

But wait, this gets exciting!

Strong's also ties, *phuō*, to *ĕmphusaō*. *Phuō*, is a prim verb that means, *to puff or blow to swell up, but only used in the implied sense to **germinate, grow, sprout or produce**…literally and figuratively **to spring up*** (Strong's 5453).

God created man and then breathed life into him. God told man to be *fruitful, multiply, fill* the earth, *subdue* it and *rule* over it. God *"put"* man into position in Eden and appointed him to tend it.

Jesus Christ, thousands of years later, *breathed* on the disciples with a breath that *fixed their position* in HIM and carried within the breath the *ability to grow and produce*.

Followers of Jesus Christ are to be fruitful (grow, flourish), we are to multiply (increase), fill the earth (replenish the holy things), subdue (fix anything that is not in God's order) and rule as God intended us to rule.

> *"For God so loved the world that He gave His only begotten Son, that whoever believes in Him should not perish but have everlasting life."* (John 3:16)

Man and Woman are restored to their original state when they accept Jesus Christ as their Lord and Savior, they are able to "eat" from the Tree of Life.

Restore is also defined as, *to renew or re-establish after interruption.*

God has and continues to fulfill His Word. God is consistent in who He is. He has not and will not deviate from His plan of redemption and restoration.

It does not matter how many interruptions you may have had in your life; God is bigger than any interruption. It does not matter how bad the things were that you may have done; God's love far outshines any bad thing done. Ultimately, it does not matter what other people have said about you or done to you; let God deal with them.

God, through Jesus Christ, always has a plan of redemption and restoration — for you and for anyone else who pursues it.

The choice is yours.

Chapter 8

Reflection

1. What are you struggling with about God?
___
___
___
___

2. Are you allowing the actions of others to determine your beliefs about God?
___
___
___
___

3. How much have the actions of others impacted your belief in or about God?
___
___
___
___

4. What thoughts do you have about the consequences of knowing good and evil?
___
___
___
___
___
___

5. What do you imagine the world would be like if Mankind lived forever?

_____
_____
_____
_____
_____

6. Why do you think God did not want Mankind to know good and evil?

_____
_____
_____
_____
_____

7. What are your thoughts regarding God removing Mankind from the Garden of Eden?

_____
_____
_____
_____
_____

The Old Testament reveals God unfolding His plan of redemption.

8. How does this change how you interpret the Old Testament?

_____
_____
_____
_____
_____

The Old Testament reveals the consequences of living by man's standard or God's standard.

9. How does this affect the need to study and learn from the Old Testament?

_____
_____
_____
_____
_____

God has not, nor will He, remove humanity's freewill to choose.

10. What are the implications of this Truth?

_____
_____
_____
_____
_____
_____
_____

11. How does it explain evil, or why bad things happen to good people?

_____
_____
_____
_____
_____

God told Man and Woman not to eat from the Tree of Knowledge of Good and Evil, one requirement.

God sent Jesus Christ to redeem humanity from the consequences of humanity's rebellion. Redemption, reconciliation to God and forgiveness of sin is only found through belief in Jesus Christ, one requirement.

12. What do you think about God's requirement?

_____
_____
_____
_____
_____

13. Why do you think He made a requirement to receive redemption?

_____
_____
_____
_____

Jesus proclaims that if you know Him, you know the Father.

14. What does the life of Jesus Christ reveal about the Father? If you do not know what Jesus Christ was like when He was on earth, read about the following encounters Jesus had with others. Then, write down what you think they are revealing about Jesus and the Father.

_____
_____
_____
_____
_____
_____
_____

Matthew 4:22-24:

_____
_____
_____
_____
_____
_____
_____
_____

Matthew 15:27-29:

_____
_____
_____
_____
_____
_____
_____
_____

Luke 22:41-46:

_____
_____
_____
_____
_____
_____
_____

Luke 22:49-51:

John 4:7-26:

John 20 reveals a beautiful experience between Jesus and Woman, Mary Magdalene.
Both Man and Woman saw two different — but very important — signs of Jesus' resurrection and His return.

15. Why do you think God allowed them to see two different things?

Mary turned and saw a man. She thought he was the gardener.

16. Why is this important to note in the story?

Mary had spent numerous hours with Jesus.

17. Why do you think she did not recognize him?

_____
_____
_____
_____
_____
_____

Mary did not recognize it was Jesus until He said her name.

18. What does this mean to you?

_____
_____
_____
_____
_____
_____

Jesus told Mary not to cling to Him, as He had not ascended into heaven. Later, when He appeared to others, He ate with them, and they touched Him.

19. What do think caused God to interrupt Jesus' ascension into heaven for Mary?

_____
_____
_____
_____
_____
_____

20. What could she have been doing that would have caused God to allow this interaction between Jesus and Mary?

_____
_____
_____
_____
_____
_____

21. What assignment did Jesus give Mary?

_____
_____
_____
_____
_____

22. Why is this important?

_____
_____
_____
_____
_____

Peter had denied knowing Jesus Christ three times. God has an angel tell the women who were at Jesus' tomb to tell the disciples to go to Galilee. The angel mentions Peter by name.

23. What does this reveal about God's heart towards redemption?

_____
_____
_____
_____
_____
_____
_____

John 21, Jesus Christ and Peter are having breakfast. Jesus asked Peter a question three times.

24. What was the question and how does the same question slightly change?

_____
_____
_____
_____
_____

25. When Peter responded, what did Jesus tell Peter to do?

26. Why do you think Jesus asked this of Peter three times?

Reconciliation and redemption only come through the belief in Jesus Christ. Transformation comes from following Him.

27. Why do you think God places this requirement on humanity?

28. How does this align with a philosophy that teaches, "many roads lead to God"?

29. Who is responsible for how you live your life here on earth?

30. Who is responsible for how others live their life here on earth?

31. Why is it important to know who is ultimately responsible for the choices they make regarding their life?

Other Revelations:

Chapter 9

The Freedom of Submission

A submitted lifestyle is not just for Woman; it applies to Man too. I wanted to clearly state this truth before any Woman slams this book shut. Submission, to submit, has been distorted, misunderstood, and misused to justify the incorrect suppression and devaluing of Woman. It has also been misused towards others.

The misapplication and abuse of submit has subjected Woman to "justified" abuse; she is my wife, my property, I can do what I will — which is not Biblical. A lack of understanding submission has been used to disqualify, thereby hindering Women who have been equipped by God to lead.

It has wounded, caused confusion in Woman's identity, pushed Woman to breaking points, and has escalated the consequences of the first rebellion, that Woman would desire to take, not just her husband, but Man, by the throat, throw him away and take his place.

Submit has become an ugly term in today's culture. But when you understand the why, how, and to whom God instructs humanity to live a submitted life to, you can find incredible freedom and peace.

Why is it so difficult for humanity to live a submitted life?

For Man and Woman, pride ranks high on the list. But pride, for many people, is a manifestation of deeper struggles. It is difficult to submit when you have been disappointed, abused, manipulated, abandoned, degraded, or devalued by someone in authority, or someone who was meant to be trustworthy, and supposed to protect but instead harmed.

Self-preservation is a defense mechanism meant to protect ourselves from others. We convince ourselves that if we refuse to submit to anyone or anything, we will not be disappointed or hurt. The reality is, submission, in some degree, is part of life. We all submit to someone or something. You can choose to submit of your own freewill, or sooner or later, something will cause you to submit your life to: wounds, work, alcohol, pornography, social media status, video games, scrolling on the phone, isolation, constant binge watching, over- or under eating, drugs, shopping, image maintenance addictions, the latest *"cause."* to name a few.

Man tends to struggle with submission out of a fear of being perceived as weak. The reality is, a Man who appropriately submits his life as God has asked of him, is an extremely strong, capable, caring, and confident Man.

Woman struggles with submission out of a fear of becoming irrelevant, useless, and confined. The reality is, a Woman who appropriately submits her life as God has asked of her, is a strategic, influential Woman of excellence.

Submit, to yield, resign or surrender to the power, will or authority of another; to yield one's opinion to the opinion or authority of another; to yield without murmuring.

Submission, the act of yielding to power or authority; obedience; compliance with the commands or laws of a superior; a yielding of one's will to the will or appointment of a superior without murmuring.

Oh, my goodness those are difficult definitions to swallow! Let us press on before I change my mind about this chapter. Yes, I am kidding. I have learned that God-ordained submission is liberating, purposeful, and keeps my life in order…which I really appreciate. However, in all transparency, the murmuring can still be a bit of a challenge for me.

To be clear, forced submission is NOT the submission God has set into place. Anything forced through physical, mental, or spiritual means, is control/abuse and it is evil. I have not found one instance where God forced anyone to do anything.

True submission is an *intentional decision to willingly set yourself into the position God has established for you.*

For you to be able to do that, you must be redeemed and restored by Jesus Christ. You do not have to have your act all together; you simply must be **steadfast** to the new lifestyle following Jesus Christ requires of you. Yes, requires of you. The promises of God are obtained through choosing to live by God's commandments. Jesus Christ showed us how to do just that.

Submit, Submitted, Submitting and a few usages of *Subjection* come from the same Greek words, but depending upon their application, have different prim roots. The variance in their prim roots brings into further clarity its intended meaning. I will provide those that are relevant to the references I provide from the Word of God.

Submit, Submitted, Submitting, Subjection, hupŏtassō, from 5259 and 5021; to subordinate; to obey, be under obedience (Strong's 5293).

Hup-ŏ, **under** or **beneath**, inferior position or condition, and specifically, **covertly** or **moderately** (Strong's 5259, emphasis added).

> *Covertly,* **secretly; closely; in private**; insidiously.
> *Moderately,* temperately, calmly; **without violence of passion.**

Tassō, to **arrange in an orderly manner** (Strong's 5021, emphasis added).

Let us place the ones above that can have a negative implication in the right perspective.

Hup-ŏ, inferior position or condition. *Inferior,* lower in place, station, age, or rank in life; lower in excellence or value.

A ruby tends to be lower, inferior, in price than a diamond, but its beauty is just as brilliant. Submission is referring to position or state of condition of something material, never the worth of an individual or a devaluing of the position they hold.

Luke 7 tells the story of Jesus Christ healing a centurion's servant.

A centurion was a Roman solider responsible for about 100 men. This reveals he was well-trained, entrusted with power and authority, had a degree of wealth, and held a respected position. He had a servant who was sick, so he asked for help. This shows he was concerned with the well-being of those under his care, and he was humble enough to ask for help. The centurion knew his own position, but showed great respect, knowledge and understanding of Jesus' position.

> *"Lord do not trouble Yourself, for **I am not worthy that You should enter <u>under</u> my roof. Therefore I did not even think myself worthy to come to You.** But say the word, and my servant will be healed. For I also am **a man placed <u>under</u> authority**, having soldiers <u>**under**</u> me. And I say to one, 'Go,' and he goes; and to another, 'Come,' and he comes; and to my servant, 'Do this,' and he does it." (Luke 7:6a-8, emphasis added)*

The word *"under"* in each of these instances is *hup-ŏ*. This story does not give any implication that the centurion felt he was an inferior individual. He knew his position. He was confident in what authority he was *"under"* and who was *"under"* his authority. He also clearly recognized that Jesus held authority that was above his, even though Jesus Christ was not a Roman.

The humility and strength of this leader is revealed in the usage of the word worthy in this statement, *"I did not even think myself worthy to come to You."* This man could easily and legally arrest, imprison, or even kill an individual with a word. He could have used his Roman authority and position to have Jesus brought to him. Yet, he did not deem himself, ENTITLED or fit, to come to Jesus in person.

How many of us have an attitude of entitlement? Today, demands are made of God, Jesus Christ, and others in the belief one is inherently deserving of certain privileges and special treatment, regardless of behavior.

Entitlement has no place in a follower of Christ's mind or heart. God does not owe us anything. He is not obligated to do anything. He operates out of His goodness, mercy, and justice because He chooses to.

A submitted life respects the value and position of others. A submitted life recognizes the wisdom of things *being arranged in an orderly fashion.* A Chief Executive Officer holds a superior position to a Director in an organization. The superior position carries more responsibility, but the person holding the position does not have more value as an individual than the inferior position. The inferior position holds important responsibility as well. Without one, the other has more difficulty carrying out their responsibilities. Submission to the flow of the organization manages the workload and brings clarity to each person's role.

A pastor in a church holds a superior position in a church organization than a janitor. But whose position do you think is "inferior" when the toilets are not working properly or the air conditioning stops working? Perspective is an interesting thing.

Humanity has allowed whispers to distort the freedom, ability to focus, peace of order, and protection found in submission. We have also allowed the whispers to twist submission to be about a person's worth and identity.

Covertly, secretly; closely; in private; **insidiously** — with intention to ensnare; deceitfully; treacherously; with malicious artifice or stratagem.

Artifice, a skill acquired by science or practice.

Stratagem, to lead an army, an artifice, particularly in war; a plan or scheme for deceiving an enemy. A trick by which some advantage is intended to be obtained.

We, as followers of Christ, are not to be deceitful, treacherous, or malicious. But the enemy embodies all those traits and more. Those who do not submit their lives to Jesus Christ and His way of life tend to operate with these intentions.

Followers of Jesus Christ are in a war. There is a real enemy. He was in the Garden, whispering in Woman's ear to disobey God. Man and Woman living a submitted life can *covertly*, with the help of Jesus Christ, devise a scheme and gain an advantage over the enemy's plans in every situation.

The war is not with people. It is the battle between good, as defined by God, and evil, as defined by God.

God's redemptive plan in the Garden defeated the enemy's plans to destroy Man and Woman. God's resurrection plan defeated the enemy's plans to kill Jesus Christ at the Cross by raising Him from the dead. God's restoration of all things will defeat any enemy's plan regarding Jesus Christ's return.

Submission, God's way, is not about control, one's value, or superiority. It is about the flow of all things being done decently and in order. God is the God of order, not chaos.

True submission is done by choice. True submission defines healthy boundaries and provides focus.

Man and Woman are to submit their lives to trusting God, obeying God, worshipping God, loving others, and submitting to God-established authority.

> *"I call heaven and earth as witnesses today against you, that I have set before you life and death, blessing and cursing; therefore choose life, that both you and your descendants may live; that you may love the Lord your God, that you may obey His voice, and that you may cling to Him, for He is your life and the length of your days;"*
> (Deuteronomy 30:19-20a)

A life lived submitted to obeying God's commands leads to life. A life lived in rebellion against God's commands leads to death. The Truth of this statement is not open for dispute because God established it. You can, however, talk to God about it. He can handle discussions; in fact, He welcomes them because He created us for relationship with Him. Remember, God walked in the Garden in the cool of the evening regularly to converse with man and woman.

Submission is based in trust.

The foundation of every act of submission is trusting God above all else. Because if you do not trust God, then every other choice to submit will be based in the actions of self (self-serving or motivated to get something in return) or contingent upon the responses of others (I will submit if they act the way I want them to). Again, I am not talking about submitting to those who operate in abusive, degrading, or manipulative behaviors.

Man's and Woman's first act of submission is to God.

The moment Man or Woman accepts Jesus Christ as their Lord and Savior they are reconciled to God and redeemed from sin. It also means that Man or Woman is agreeing to forgo their personal preference of lifestyle and submit to God's way of life.

> *"So he answered and said, "'You shall love the Lord your God with all your heart, with all your soul, with all your strength, and with all your mind,'"* (Luke 10:27a)

Followers of Jesus Christ (Christians) are supposed to be committed to living their life as God has established. It is a new way of believing, thinking, and acting. Unfortunately, too many, out of desperation, "get saved" but do not submit their life to God, and they miss out on the blessings and promises of God.

The objective of all believers in Jesus Christ is to **PURSUE** living a sinless life. Man, nor Woman, can live completely sinless, that is one reason why we need Jesus. But it is possible to live free from the entanglement and bondage of sin. This process is called transformation, renewing of the mind, and it's discussed more fully in an upcoming chapter.

Trust God.

> *"As for God, His way is perfect; The word of the Lord is proven; He is a shield to all who trust in Him."* (2 Samuel 22:31)

A submitted life recognizes God's Way is perfect. His Word is proven repeatedly. He is a shield to all who trust in Him. God is patient while building trust with His children. But sooner or later, you will have to decide whether you trust Him and His commands. You must choose to live your life by His trustworthy commands, or by the shifting sands of the world's culture.

Worship God.

> *"God is Spirit, and those who worship Him must worship in spirit and truth."* (John 4:24)

Worshipping God is more than a Sunday service. It is a lifestyle spent growing in revelation, understanding, and confidence of who God is and how much He loves you. Worship is putting God first and every act being motivated by the joy of relationship with Him.

Obey God.

> *"Behold, I set before you today a blessing and a curse: the blessing, if you obey the commandments of the Lord your God which I command you today; and the curse, if you do not obey the commandments of the Lord your God, but turn aside from the way which I command you today, to go after other gods which you have not known."* (Deuteronomy 11:26-28)

God set before Mankind the choice to live a blessed or a cursed life. Obeying God will always lead to His blessing…always. Obeying God is motivated by choosing to love Him.

It is interesting to note that the word *obey* in this verse, is from the Hebrew word, *shâma'* pronounced, *shaw-mah'*.

It means, *to hear intelligently, with the implication of attention and obedience*. It further conveys the meaning to *diligently, discern, and give ear* to what is being said (Strong's 8085).

To hear intelligently, with the implication of attention and obedience.

There is no forced obeying. God is not beating His fists, stomping His feet, demanding you do exactly what He is telling you to do or else HE will personally crush you like a bug.

He is giving humanity information that says, if you do this, it will go well; if you do not, then the consequences you set in motion from your CHOICES will bring destruction and death. So, listen INTELLIGENTLY, think about it, chew on it, think logically about what God says. History has shown, and lives will ultimately reveal, His Word is True. But you must be willing to submit yourself, tap down that pride, fear, insecurity, and the desire to control everything and see God has a better way.

Diligently discern.

Discern what? Discern between what is good and what is evil. God is teaching humanity the difference between good and evil. Yes, humanity's eyes were opened to the knowledge of good and evil. But humanity must be taught what is good and what is evil…again, by God's standard, not humanity's. Hence, The Ten Commandments.

> *"But this is what I commanded them, saying, 'Obey My voice, and I will be your God, and you shall be My people. And walk in all the ways that I have commanded you, that it may be well with you.'"* (Jeremiah 7:23, Old Testament)

> *"If you keep My commandments, you will abide in My love, just as I have kept My Father's commandments and abide in His love."* (John 15:10, New Testament)

Jesus, the Son of God, lived and lives a submitted life. He submits His Will to the Father's Will. He worships the Father, and He obeys the Father…through a relationship of trust and love.

One of my favorite revelations about a relationship with Almighty God is given by Jesus Himself at a most vulnerable moment. Jesus Christ, who knew what He would endure from the beginning in Genesis 3, is having an intimate, real, heart-wrenching, conversation with His Father.

> *"And He was withdrawn from them about a stone's throw, and He knelt down and prayed, saying, "Father, if it is Your will, take this cup away from Me; nevertheless not My will, but Yours, be done." Then an angel appeared to Him from heaven, strengthening Him."* (Luke 22:41-43)

This showed me I can go to the Father and talk to Him about the doubts, challenges, the hard stuff of life. I can be open and honest with Him about questions and the struggle to work through something. He is there with me in the cool of the evening or whatever time of day it is. He is in the midst. But the outcome is still submission to the Father's instructions.

Therefore, relationship-based submission is an act of respect, honor, and love (appropriate to the type of relationship).

Man's and Woman's second act of submission is to God-given authority.

Governmental Authority

Man and Woman are to submit themselves to governmental authority, to honor God. It is always positional. You may or may not like the personality of the person God has allowed in a position of authority. That is not relevant.

> **"Let every soul** *be subject to the governing authorities. For there is no authority except from God, and the authorities that exist are appointed by God. Therefore whoever resists the authority resists the ordinance of God, and those who resist will bring judgment on themselves."* (Romans 13:1-2, emphasis added)

Without structure, there is chaos. There are structural systems in place so order can be administered and maintained. Structure requires submission to produce productivity. An outcome is lives lived in peace.

Without godly men and women in position of authority, there will be bondage and heavy burdens.

1 Samuel 8 not only shows that God never intended humanity to have people RULE over them, but also forewarned them of what will happen when ungodly "kings" are ruling.

> *"Then all the elders of Israel gathered together and came to Samuel at Ramah, and said to him, "Look, you are old, and your sons do not walk in your ways. Now* **make us a king to judge us like all the nations."** (vs. 4,5, emphasis added)

> *"So Samuel prayed to the Lord. And the Lord said to Samuel, "Heed the voice of the people in all that they say to you; for they have not rejected you,* **but they have rejected Me, that I should not reign over them."** (vs. 6b,7, emphasis added)

> *"Now therefore, heed their voice. However, you shall* **solemnly forewarn them**, *and show them the behavior of the king who will reign over them."* (vs 9, emphasis added)

> *"And he said, "This will be the behavior of the king who will reign over you:* **He will take** *your sons and appoint them for his own chariots and to be his horsemen, and some will run before his chariots. He will appoint captains over his thousands and captains over his fifties, will set some to plow his ground and reap his harvest, and some to make his weapons of war and equipment for his chariots.* **He will take your daughters** *to be perfumers, cooks, and bakers. And* **he will take the best of your fields, your vineyards, and your olive groves,** *and give them to his servants.* **He will take a tenth of your grain** *and your vintage, and give it to his officers and servants. And* **he will take** *your male servants, your female servants, your finest young men, and your donkeys,* **and <u>put</u> <u>them</u> <u>to</u> <u>his</u> <u>work</u>***. He will take a tenth of your sheep. And <u>you</u> <u>will</u> <u>be</u> <u>his</u> <u>servants</u>."* (vs. 11-17, emphasis added)

And humanity's response after God told them not once, but twice, the consequences of what they were asking for:

> *"They said, "No, but we will have a king over us,* **that we also may be like all the nations,** *and that our king may judge us and go out before us and fight our battles."*

God did not rescue them, not yet anyway. He did not put His foot down and say no. He did not enable them. He had created them with freewill, with the ability to hear intelligently, to reason, and to decide for themselves. God submitted His Will to their will, but He did not relinquish who He was or His rightful place. He turned them over to what they said they wanted…and the bondage it would create.

> *"So the Lord said to Samuel, "Heed their voice, and make them a king."* (vs 22)

A Man or Woman of God is not shaken by whoever is in positions of authority, for they know their trust is in the Lord. They are confident God is more than able to work His plan through any decision of Mankind. They know God is more than able to deliver, protect, provide, and bless them, and even if He allows them to perish, they are still resting in confident peace that eternity with Him is a place of BLISS.

God, because He created humanity to rule over the earth, allows humanity to set up structures to govern. He works in and through those individuals to govern.

Those individuals choose to govern from His commands, which brings life to all, or through their own personal gain, which puts people into bondage. Ultimately, God works ALL things to His Will, which is the return of Jesus Christ to rule and reign over all.

Followers of Jesus Christ are not only to submit to governing authorities, but to pray for them.

> *"Therefore I exhort first of all that supplications, prayers, intercessions, and giving of thanks be made for all men, for kings and all who are in authority, that we may lead a quiet and peaceable life in all godliness and reverence. For this is good and acceptable in the sight of God our Savior,"* (1 Timothy 2:1-3)

The choice of submission and prayer for the governmental authorities over us honors God and positions us for God's promises to be evident in our lives…regardless of who holds the office.

> *Therefore submit yourselves to every ordinance of man **for the Lord's sake**, whether to the king as supreme, or to governors, as to those who are sent by him for the punishment of evildoers and for the praise of those who do good. **For this is the will of God, that by doing good you may put to silence the ignorance of foolish men — as free,** yet not using liberty as a cloak for vice, but as bondservants of God."*
> (1 Peter 2:13-16, emphasis added)

Followers of Christ choose to submit to governmental authority for the Lord's sake. As one who is free in Christ Jesus, we know that our peace and security is not in another person, but in the One who holds all authority. God will use the submission of those who follow His commands to silence ignorance. It might take a while, but sooner or later, God's Truth will prevail. It always has, and it always will.

Remember, it is not submission, and your prayers are not effective, if you are murmuring, complaining, or bad mouthing an individual to others, on social media…or even when you are alone.

Church Authority

Followers of Christ are to submit to those who are in spiritual leadership over us. They are the ones who are called by God to watch over our souls, and they must give an account to God — not to you — on how they did.

> *"Obey those who rule over you, and be submissive, for they watch out for your souls, as those who must give account. Let them do so with joy and not with grief, for that would be unprofitable for you."* (Hebrews 13:17)

I believe it is wonderful many Apostles, Prophets, Evangelists, Pastors, and Teachers are using media platforms to get the Word of God to the corners of the world. However, when it comes to Joyce Meyer or Priscilla Shirer, as wonderful teachers they are, I do not submit to them as my Church (Spiritual) Authority. They do not know me, and I do not know them. Remember, God is all about relationship!

I am firmly committed to a local church. I have a Pastor. He and his wife are who I submit to as my church authority. They know me, and I know them. My church is part of a larger fellowship. I choose to submit to the governing authorities over this fellowship. I am responsible for my part, not theirs. God holds each of us responsible for our individual choices in aligning our lives with His commands.

Submission is not blindness. Submission to governmental and church authorities is not about being blindly led and not taking any personal responsibility for oneself. Every person will stand before God and give an account of their life. Excuses for not trusting God did not work for the Man or Woman in the Garden of Eden, and they will not work for anyone else.

I respect, through my submission, the decisions that my Pastor or church leadership makes. I believe they love the Lord; they are studying the Scriptures, praying, and have more information about situations than I do. So, if it does not violate Scripture, I follow. If it involves another person, and I am not directly involved in the situation, I am not to be a busybody (1 Peter 4:15), nor be a gossiper (Proverbs 16:28), nor be idle and say things I should not (1 Timothy 5:13). I am to trust God is more than able to work out all things.

Submit to One Another

The Holy Bible is written for every person in the world. The instruction being given is to those who are seeking after and following God, however imperfectly that may be.

Followers of Christ are to submit to each other.

> *"speaking to one another in psalms and hymns and spiritual songs, singing and making melody in your heart to the Lord, giving thanks always for all things to God the Father in*

the name of our Lord Jesus Christ, **submitting to one another in the fear of God**.*"* (Ephesians 5:19-21, emphasis added)

Ephesians was written to the fledging local church. So, the letter's audience were fellow followers of Christ. Followers of Christ submit to other followers of Christ. It puts a deeper understanding of Jesus' words, *"By this all will know that you are My disciples, if you have love for one another"* (John 13:35).

We are to serve, support and encourage one another. John 13 gives the beautiful account of how every follower of Christ should pursue serving one another. This is a reflection of submission. Jesus Christ, Son of God, who healed, delivered, endured a brutal death who now sits at the right hand of the Father, knelt down and washed other people's nasty, dirty, smelly feet.

Jesus Christ, who holds a superior position to us all, submitted to an inferior position and showed us all how to serve and love. The washing of the followers' feet did not diminish His identity. It did not lessen His worth. It did not impede His purpose. Jesus Christ submitted Himself to the Father's Will, and that included showing His followers how to live, in submission to one another.

Wives Submit to Husbands

Women are not instructed by the Holy Bible to submit to Men other than in the context above (brotherly and sisterly love). The Word of God instructs that wives are to submit to their husbands. This brings order to the follower of Christ's home. Husband and Wife are equal partners in a relationship designed by God to bring companionship. The Husband and the Wife contribute different but necessary qualities to make a house a home and a group of people a family.

The word *obey,* by its known definition, *to comply with the commands, orders or instructions of a superior,* is not used in married relationships. It is only used in parent / child and master / slave relationships. Do not take offense. The reality is, throughout the history of humanity, all ethnicities have been subjected to slavery. It is an evil of humanity's doing, not God's. God has worked in and through the evil of slavery. God has always raised up brave men and women of all ethnicities to subdue the evil of slavery.

Colossians 3:18-21 give instruction on how followers of Christ should conduct themselves within their home.

> *Wives, submit to your own husbands, as is fitting in the Lord.* (verse 18)
> *Husbands, love your wives and do not be bitter toward them.* (verse 19)
> *Children, obey your parents in all things, for this is well pleasing to the Lord.* (verse 20)
> *Fathers, do not provoke your children, lest they become discouraged.* (verse 21)

A Man is to leave his father and mother and be joined to his Wife and become one flesh (Genesis 2:24). This is so much more than sexual intimacy. A Husband and Wife are to live in spiritual, emotional, mental, and physical intimacy, basically naked towards each other...***without any shame.*** This is impossible without God at the center of each spouse's life and as the center of the marriage. Marriage requires work even when God is in the midst, and it is worth the tending and keeping marriage requires.

Do you recall the arch? Man and Woman facing each other, hands above their heads, pressing against each other, forming an arch. If one is out of place, or does not apply equal strength, the other falls.

The word "love" used for Husbands to love their wife, is the same love used when Jesus references His love for us or how all believers are to love God. When a husband loves his wife with the purity of this type of love, it is easy for a wife to submit to, to respect, her husband.

Woman, you have the ability within you to encourage and equip men to be the *Ish* they are created to be. A Man who embraces the destiny God breathed into him can love and protect as he was intended. What fulfillment and joy of knowing that you were a part of encouraging the greatness within a Man, and he was then able to love a fellow sister as the treasure she is. What an impact and legacy that would be!

Every act of submission — government authority, church authority, toward other followers of Christ, and Wife to Husband — is the exact same definition of submit. It is not mindless obedience. It does not devalue nor negate the importance of the contributions each person makes to the whole.

Submission is a choice Man and Woman make as an act of honoring and trusting the Lord.

Submission puts things in order. We all have a deep desire to have things in order, not control, but in proper, liberating, freeing, and peaceful order.

Exceptions to Submission

There are stories in the Bible where people chose not to submit in the areas listed above. They are in the Bible so we would learn when it is appropriate to disobey and to prepare us for the possible consequences of our disobedience.

Each of these stories also reveals a mindset already established before they were faced with very difficult situations. In each of these instances, there was not ranting, bad-mouthing, finger-pointing, disrespect towards a person, justification of actions, or degrading behavior towards self or anyone else. There was a simple, quiet, resolute commitment to how they governed their lives.

Ultimately, it revealed their trust in God, no matter the consequence.

Governmental Exceptions

It is appropriate to refuse to submit to government authority when the governing entity asks you to violate God's Sovereignty, including His commands.

Exodus 1:15-19 tells the story of how the king of Egypt ordered the midwives to kill the male babies when they are born. The midwives feared God, valued life, and chose to save them. God dealt well with the midwives and provided households for them. Because of their efforts, a leader was saved that led millions out of slavery.

Joshua 2 tells the story of a prostitute, Rahab, who went against Jericho's king, and hid the spies. Rahab had heard what God had done before and she believed God. She defied direct orders from Jericho's king at great risk to herself and those in her household. God saved her and her family, and Rahab is in the genealogy of Jesus Christ.

Daniel 6 tells the story of a conspiracy against Daniel because of jealousy. Other advisors knew that Daniel was faithful to his service to God, through prayer, worship, and thanksgiving. They devised a plan that would trap Daniel in his worship of the Lord. Daniel knew of the penalty he would pay if he continued in his prayer and worship of God. He did it anyway because he loved and trusted God more than he feared the king. God delivered Daniel, exalted him, and the king sent a decree to the nation that the God of Daniel was the one true God.

I cannot imagine the thoughts that went through each of these people when they were faced with life and death choices. They trusted God regardless of the outcome. We often want God to remove us from situations, but He let Daniel get thrown into the lion's den.

Employer / Employee Submission

Shadrach, Meshach and Abed-Nego were colleagues of Daniel. These four men were captives, slaves, who served before the king of Babylon. They were taken from their homes, trained for at least three years, and then put to work for the king. But they never forgot who they truly worked for.

Daniel 3 reveals the difficulty an employee faces when an employer asks them to do something that violates God's commands. King Nebuchadnezzar had a large statue of himself built and commanded that when you heard music, you were to fall down and worship the image. The consequence for anyone who refused to do was to be thrown into a fiery furnace.

Shadrach, Meshach and Abed-Nego were tattled on by arrogant and jealous co-workers. The king, furious, went to them and in his accusation made this interesting statement, *"And who is the god who will deliver you from my hands?"* (Daniel 3:15b)

Really chew on Shadrach's, Meshach's, and Abed-Nego's response to the king.

> *Shadrach, Meshach, and Abed-Nego answered and said to the king, "O Nebuchadnezzar,* ***we have no need to answer you in this matter****. If that is the case,* ***our God whom we serve is able to deliver us*** *from the burning fiery furnace, and* ***He will deliver us from your hand****, O king.* **But if not**, *let it be known to you, O king, that* __we do not serve your gods,__ __nor will we worship the gold image__ *which you have set up."* (Daniel 3:16-18, emphasis added)

These three men had already determined in their hearts, LONG BEFORE this incident, who their God was, and who they truly served. They knew God was able to deliver them from the fire and from the king. But, more than that, they still trusted in Him if He chose to let them perish in the fire.

God allowed them to be put into the fire. Today, we often pray to be delivered at the first sign of trouble. But God, He met them in the midst of the fire. A slightly different location than the cool of the evening, but the result is the same. God is in the midst.

You must decide to live your life submitted to God above all else before you are faced with such a choice. You probably will not get thrown into a literal fire, but you may get fired through your refusal to compromise.

God will always redeem those who put their trust in Him. If you agree to commit an act that is against God's commands, then you have submitted your life to another's control, in ways far beyond that initial incident.

Church Authority (Religious Leaders)

There is a time when it is appropriate not to submit to the leaders of a church or denomination. There is also a Scriptural way to go about it.

Acts 4 tells the story when the Sadducees (Religious Leaders) were quite unhappy that the disciples were teaching about Jesus Christ and His resurrection from the dead. The leadership commanded Peter and John *"not to speak at all nor teach in the name of Jesus."* (Acts 4:18)

Peter and John's response was similar to Daniel and his friends. They told leadership, *"Whether it is right in the sight of God to listen to you more than to God, you judge. For we cannot but speak the things which we have seen and heard."* (Acts 4:19-20) Then, Peter and John prayed for more boldness to preach Jesus Christ.

Peter and John were not disrespectful of leadership. They spoke directly to them, stated their position, and then went about their business. They did not gossip, slander, spread rumors, or maliciously cause division. They did not say one thing to them, then went away and did another.

The Church has the responsibility to worship God, preach Jesus Christ, be led by the Holy Spirit, and pursue abiding by the Word of God. The Church is meant to be a place of corporate worship, equipping of the people of God for the work of the ministry, restoration, and fellowship.

If your church leadership is not adhering to the commands of God, in word and in deed, then you should seriously consider finding another home church to be planted in. The Standard is the Holy Bible, all of it, not just bits and pieces. It matters not if it makes people uncomfortable, confrontation of sin in all our lives is uncomfortable. But I imagine pain, anger, bitterness, hatred, and, ultimately, hell are significantly more uncomfortable.

There is a difference between being made uncomfortable because the Word of God is renewing and transforming your mind and the spirit of offense. Offense is rampant today, and it is destructive.

Do not leave a church because you get offended. Deal with the emotion of offense. God is the One who calls you to a local church for a purpose. He, through grace, will transition you when He needs you to move.

The Holy Bible gives clear instruction on how to handle issues and disagreements…you go directly to the person, face-to-face.

Husband and Wife Submission

There are Biblical examples of situations when a wife should not submit to her husband's decision, request, or action. A husband, who loves his wife as Jesus Christ loves the Church, would never ask his wife to do unscriptural, immoral, or illegal acts. That is why is it is important to marry someone who believes in and follows Jesus Christ.

Husbands are human; therefore, they might misjudge a situation. 1 Samuel 25 gives such an example. David, God's anointed king, was passing through the land. He sent messengers to Nabal, whom David had previously protected his belongings, to ask him for whatever he would be willing to contribute to the feast. Nabal ignored the request. Nabal's servant told Abigail, Nabal's wife, what had transpired. Abigail quickly made preparations, intercepted David on the road, profusely apologized, and gave him provisions for the feast.

Abigail's actions saved Nabal's household.

She then went back to tell her husband what she had done — submission. Nabal was *"harsh and evil in his doings."* Life could not have been easy for Abigail. She knew that her actions could cause her great harm by her husband. But she was a woman of *"good understanding,"* and chose to do what was right.

I am not justifying nor excusing abuse. There is none. Abuse is by Man or Woman's freewill. It is not, nor will ever be, God's Will.

But doing the right, the Godly thing comes with consequences. Wisdom dictates you understand those consequences and trust God through them all. He always works things out. Always.

Faithfulness in Disobedience

Every follower of Christ's submission is to the Lord above all else. Therefore, there will be faithfulness to the Lord found in disobeying those who are in God-ordained authority over you. This disobedience is not based in emotional responses or even in the severity of the situation. Disobedience in submission is only justified when it violates God's commands. Read, study, and pursue to live The Ten Commandments. If you are asked to do something that violates them, then you know what your response should be.

Submission is a freedom.

Submission frees Man and Woman to operate in their God-given position. It removes the distractions of what is other people's responsibility and allows you to focus on what is your purpose and responsibility. Others may not be doing their part, according to how you think they should, but let go and let God work it out with them. He is much better at it than we are.

Submission brings order.

There is too much drama and offense in the world. It is exhausting. Submission removes the drama from your life, and it can also remove the offense. A life submitted to God is an orderly, peace-filled, fulfilling, purpose-driven life.

One of my favorite verses is found in 1 Thessalonians 4. I believe it speaks to a submitted life for a follower of Jesus Christ.

> *But **concerning brotherly love** you have no need that I should write to you, for you yourselves are **taught by God to love one another**; and indeed you do so toward all the brethren who are in all Macedonia. But we urge you, brethren, that **you increase more and more**; that you also **aspire to lead a quiet life**, to **mind your own business**, and to **work with your own hands**, as we commanded you, that you may **walk properly toward those who are outside**, and that **you may lack nothing.** (1 Thessalonians 4:9-12, emphasis added)*

A quiet life does not mean lack in any form. A quiet life is a full life. It is a life filled with peace, joy, productivity, and influence. It is the fruit of a life lived submitted to the Lord and His commands.

God is the God of order, not chaos. Women have a deep desire for things to be in order. A Woman submitted to the order of God brings His order into the situation. A Woman attempting to bring order into a situation without submitting to God will only bring frustration, exhaustion, and chaos.

Choose to submit. Choose to position yourself to flow in the goodness of God.

Chapter 9

Reflection

A submitted lifestyle is for both Man and Woman as a follower of Jesus Christ.

1. What are your thoughts regarding a submitted way of life?

___

2. What is your perception of submit?

___

3. Why is submission an ugly term today?

___

4. What makes submission difficult for people?

___

5a. What makes submission difficult for Men?

_____
_____
_____
_____
_____

5b. Are there other reasons you can think of regarding Man's difficulty in submitting his life to the Lord or to others?

_____
_____
_____
_____
_____
_____
_____

6a. What makes submission difficult for Women?

_____
_____
_____
_____
_____

6b. Are there other reasons you can think of regarding Woman's difficulty in submitting her life to the Lord or to others?

_____
_____
_____
_____
_____
_____
_____

7. What is the definition of submit?

_____
_____
_____
_____
_____

8. What is the definition of submission?

9a. What part of those definitions did you think, "Well, that is not happening?"

9b. Why?

10. Is the type of submission we are talking about forced?

Write down your thoughts about this truth.

11. Why is true submission a choice?

___

Submit, Submitted, Submitting, Subjection, hupŏtassō, from 5259 and 5021; to subordinate; to obey, be under obedience (Strong's 5293).

Hup-ŏ, **under** or **beneath**, inferior position or condition, and specifically, **covertly** or **moderately** (Strong's 5259, emphasis added).

Tassō, to **arrange in an orderly manner** (Strong's 5021, emphasis added).

12. What are some of the things that come to your mind when you read through the definition nuances of submit?

___

Read the story of the centurion in Luke 7.

13. How does this story give a better understanding of how submit puts thing in order?

___

14a. Does submit, in any of the instances, lessen the value or importance of an individual?

___

159

14b. Why or why not?

True submission is a conscience decision to properly align oneself to God and His commands.

15. What is the first step of submitting to God's plan of reconciliation and redemption?

16. What is being submitted and to whom?

17. What is the objective of every follower of Jesus Christ?

18. What are the three aspects of submitting one's life to God?

19. How does a submitted life show trust in God?

_____
_____
_____
_____
_____

20. How does a submitted life reveal honoring God?

_____
_____
_____
_____
_____

21. How does a submitted life reflect obedience to God?

_____
_____
_____
_____
_____

Obey, **shâmaʿ** *shaw-mah, to hear intelligently, with the implication of attention and obedience.* It further conveys the meaning to *diligently, discern, and give ear* to what is being said (Strong's 8085).

22. How does this definition of obey change your perspective regarding obey?

_____
_____
_____
_____
_____

23. How does it change how you view God?

_____
_____
_____

24. How does it impact your responsibility in obeying God's commands?

___

"If you keep My commandments, you will abide in My love, just as I have kept My Father's commandments and abide in His love." (John 15:10)

Jesus Christ lived His life submitted to the Father.

25. How does His life reflect what true submission is?

___

Read John 15:10 again.

26. What emotion is in the mix of submission?

___

Man and Woman are to submit to God-given authority. (1 Timothy 2:1-3, 1 Peter 2:13-16)

27. Why are Man and Woman to submit to God-given authority?

___

28. Why is it important to submit to God-given authority?

29. Who has given leadership authority?

30. What else are followers of Christ to do for those in authority?

Followers of Jesus Christ are to submit to Church Leadership.

31. Why do followers of Christ submit to their local church leadership?

32. Why is it important to submit to local church leadership?

33a. Is submission done with blinders on our eyes?

33b. Why or why not?

34. How is submission manifested in the local church? (Galatians 5:13-14; 1 Peter 3:8-9)

Followers Submit to Other Followers of Jesus Christ

35. What example does it show when followers of Christ submit to other followers?

36. What are some examples of submitting to one another?

37. How did Jesus Christ show what it means to submit oneself to one another? (John 13)

Wives Are to Submit to Their Husband

38. Why do you think a wife is to submit to her husband?

39. Does submitting to a husband lessen the value and worth of a wife?

40. Does submitting to a husband devalue the contributions a wife brings to the marriage?

41. Does the term obey, in its strictest definition, *to comply with the commands, orders or instructions of a superior,* apply to the marriage relationship?

Colossians 3:18-21 arranges the family unit in an orderly fashion. This removes chaos, provides safety, and is held together by love.

> *Wives, submit to your own husbands, as is fitting in the Lord.* (verse 18)
> *Husbands, love your wives and do not be bitter toward them.* (verse 19)
> *Children, obey your parents in all things, for this is well pleasing to the Lord.* (verse 20)
> *Fathers, do not provoke your children, lest they become discouraged.* (verse 21)

42. Write down your thoughts about the instructions Colossians 3:18-21 provide for us.

_____
_____
_____
_____
_____

43. How well does your family function in this flow?

_____
_____
_____
_____
_____

44. What can you personally do about your role in the family unit?

_____
_____
_____
_____
_____

45. How does one person's actions affect another person's role?

_____
_____
_____
_____
_____

46. Married or not, there is wisdom in God's instructions. What can you learn from these verses?

___

There are Biblically based exceptions to submission.

Governing Authorities

Read Exodus 1:15-19.

47. What justified the midwives refusing to submit to the governing authority of the Pharaoh?

___

48. What were the midwives' reward?

___

Read Joshua 2.

49. What justified Rahab in disobeying the governing authority by not revealing the spies?

___

50. What was her reward?

Read Daniel 6.

51. What habit did Daniel have that led to his co-workers tattling on him?

52. What penalty did Daniel face if he disobeyed the law of man?

53. When did God save him and why is that important to remember?

54. What was the outcome, the fruit, of Daniel's disobedience of the king?

Employer Authority

Read Daniel 1-3.

55. Who were Shadrach, Meshach and Abed-Nego submitted to?

_____
_____
_____
_____

56. What were Shadrach, Meshach and Abed-Nego asked to do that violated their primary relationship?

_____
_____
_____
_____

Read Daniel 3:16-18.

57. Write down your thoughts regarding their choice to submit to God rather than man.

_____
_____
_____
_____

Church (Religious) Leaders

Read Acts 4.

58. What did the Sadducees tell Peter and John to stop doing?

_____
_____
_____
_____

59. Why do you think they instructed Peter and John to stop teaching about Jesus Christ?

60. Was the response Peter and John gave to the leaders rude or disrespectful?

61. Why did Peter and John refuse to submit to the command the Sadducees gave them?

62. When is it justifiable to disobey a command (directive) from church leadership?

63. What is the honorable way to disobey (disagree) with church leadership?

Husband and Wife

Read 1 Samuel 25.

64. When is it appropriate for a wife to not submit to her husband's decision?

_____
_____
_____
_____
_____

65. Will there be consequences a wife will face for not submitting to her husband's decision, even if not submitting was the right thing to do?

_____
_____
_____
_____
_____

66. What do you think makes it easier to face consequences when you refuse to submit to ungodly commands?

_____
_____
_____
_____
_____

67. Who is the ultimate One you submit your life to?

_____
_____
_____
_____
_____

68. How does this help you determine when you submit and when you do not?

69. How is a submitted life a freedom?

70. How does a submitted life bring order?

Read 1 Thessalonians 4:9-12.

71. How do these verses reveal a submitted life, a life that is properly arranged?

72. What is the fruit of a submitted life?

73. What areas of your life are not submitted according to the Lord's instructions?

___

74. What steps do you need to take in order for you to submit those areas of your life that are out of alignment with the proper order?

___

Other Revelations:

___

Chapter 10

Behold! A Virtuous Woman

The world today does not seem to want to talk about the virtue of a person, their character. The virtue of an individual appears to have little to no merit in humanity's quick handing out of judgment towards an individual. Humanity tends to lean towards the outside accomplishments, a title, a bank account or the number of followers on social media, to determine the worth of an individual.

The embodiment of your life is in direct correlation to the content of your character. One's virtue holds the key to a life lived in chaos or peace, misery or joy, emptiness or fulfillment, hatred or love. Fame, fortune, or materials things will never fill the void that cultivating a virtuous character will.

> *"And now, my daughter, do not fear. I will do for you all that you request, **for all the people** of my town **know** that you are a **virtuous** woman."* (Ruth 3:11, emphasis added)

Ruth is a short book; I encourage you to read it to get an idea of the characters in the story. Do not apply today's culture to the story. An understanding of the society and culture of the times is needed to put things in proper context. But to summarize, the primary characters are Naomi, Ruth, and Boaz. Naomi was Ruth's mother-in-law. Both Naomi and Ruth lost their husbands. Naomi returned to Bethlehem, and Ruth chose to go with her instead of returning to her people, the Moabites. Boaz was a landowner and a close relative who had the right to marry Ruth. However, there was a closer relative, so Boaz, a man of honor, had to work those things out before he could marry Ruth.

Boaz tells Ruth that the entire town knows that she is a virtuous woman. That was her reputation. She had to earn that reputation by remaining faithful and overcoming challenges with wisdom, grace, and strength.

Ruth is also one of the four women named in Jesus' genealogy in the Book of Matthew: Tamar, Rahab, Ruth, and Bathsheba — every one of these stories reveals God's power to redeem, restore, and live with great purpose, despite the things that happened to each of these women.

The outcome of their lives was contingent upon the choices they made in each situation they faced. These women faced situations, not necessarily because of their own doing, but because the choices of others impacted their lives. They are amazing women because they chose to rise above the situation…they were women of virtue.

Woman, you were created to be a virtuous Woman.

What does it mean to be a virtuous Woman? How does one become a virtuous Woman? Why should a Woman pursue cultivating a virtuous character?

Why.
You need to take a moment and at least begin to answer the "why." The answer to the "why" is what anchors, sustains and motivates you to make necessary changes, do the work, and stay the course. A portion of my "why" came from an anonymous quote: *"Someone once told me the definition of Hell: The last day you have on earth, the person you became will meet the person you **could** have become."*

I want to become all I can become. I want my life to matter and to make a difference. I have tried to live my life according my and the world's idea of living. At best, its result was unfulfilling, at its worst, heartache, depression, and emptiness.

My why is anchored in the desire to live life worthy of Almighty God, to have no regrets, to be a woman of integrity, to love others well, and to do what is within my ability to do to support, encourage, and equip others to become all they are called to.

What.
What it means to be a virtuous Woman cannot be defined by humanity. It cannot be fully defined by you either. It must first be defined by God because He nor His Truths change. This provides a stable foundation and consistent guidelines, so confusion from current culture and trends do not take you off course. You must know the end goal to know what you are working towards, making sacrifices for, and what you want to achieve.

It is difficult for an arrow to hit its target if the target keeps moving.

I have made it my ambition to cultivate within me who God has called me to be. As I cultivate the heart and mind God desires for me, everything else begins to align. Character first, then purpose is revealed.

How.

How to become and live as a virtuous Woman also cannot be defined by humanity. One does not become a medical doctor by taking music classes. A musician does not excel at her gift by focusing on what it takes to become a chef. The how is set before you through choices; those choices mold and shape your character.

I do my best to align the choices I make with God's Word, His Heart, and His Will. There are times that I miss it, but even those, because my heart is to follow Him, work out for my good… eventually.

Now, back to the "what." What is a virtuous Woman?

Virtuous, Hebrew: *chayil*, pronounced, *khah-yil*, a force, whether of men, means or other resources; an *army, wealth, virtue, valor, strength:* –able, activity (+) army, band of men (soldiers), company, (great) forces, goods, host, might, power, riches, strength, strong, substance, train, (+) valiant (-ly), valour, virtuous (ly), war, worthy (ily) (Strong's 2428 from 2342).

This word, *chayil*, is the same word used for *valour* when it is referencing mighty men who fought in armies. It denotes a force to be reckoned with. It is a force coming to help, to bring whatever resources are needed for the battle. So, it's not just one thing. It is not limited to strength, but if strength is what is needed, that is what is brought.

Remember, Man and Woman carry different types of strength. Both are necessary. Both are important. Both should be valued. They are not greater than or less than the other. They are simply different.

Judges 4-5 tells an incredible story of how the *chayil* of Man and Woman are to work together. Deborah was a judge over Israel. She was a prophetess and a wife of Lapidoth. Remember, I mentioned that every detail in the Word of God is important. I believe that one of the reasons the Holy Bible tells us that Deborah was a wife was to give us insight into the dynamics of life. She had to balance the demands of her calling (position) with the responsibilities of being a wife, and most likely, a mother.

Barak was the leader of the army. Deborah told Barak to go to battle. Barak told Deborah that he would not go if she did not go as well. Deborah told Barak that if she went with him into battle, there would be no glory for Barak. But the enemy king, Sisera, would fall at the hands of a woman (Jael). Barak's virtue is revealed that he was more concerned about winning the battle than who got the glory. A lesson for us all.

Barak was a military man. He was intelligent, well-trained, and physically very strong. Battles back then were face-to-face combat, bloody, and gruesome. They required continual training, incredible stamina, and strength. He did not need physical strength from Deborah to win the battle. He needed the resources, the strength, Deborah brought to the battle to bring about victory.

In these days, the prophet or prophetess represented the voice of God. Barak knew Deborah heard from the Lord and trusted in her character to give him the Lord's strategy to win the battle. He knew she could behold the situation from a different perspective.

Deborah went with Barak, but she did not take his identity nor his position as commander of the army. She continued to operate in her identity as *Ishah*, *Aleph*, *Shin*, *Hey,* and in her position. She added her strengths to his strengths.

Deborah and Barak above all, trusted in God. They knew their individual strengths and they understood each other's strengths. They were not in competition with each other, and they did not demean the other's strength or position. They both operated in the strength, gifts, and positions the Lord had given to them.

They also knew they needed to work together to accomplish the victory. This is an understanding we all need to keep in mind. Virtuous people work past petty differences and focus on the bigger purpose. Virtuous people do not tear others down; they see the intrinsic worth and strength others bring to accomplish wondrous things.

Virtuous encompasses *valor*, which is defined as, *strength of mind in regard to danger, that quality which enables one to encounter danger with firmness; personal bravery; courage; intrepidity; and prowess.*

You have within you the strength of mind to encounter any situation with firmness, personal bravery, courage, and boldness. You have been given by God the ability to bring aid and other resources to surround and protect those who need it…including yourself.

It takes a strength of mind, a determined mindset, to face situations and do the right thing… especially when others are telling you to go against what God is telling you to do. It takes personal bravery to be kind toward someone who has wronged you. It takes tremendous strength to encounter any type of danger and stand for right, mercy, and justice when others will not or cannot.

The attributes that define a virtuous Woman do not just happen. Once they are known, they must be developed until they become a part of your nature. They become how you feel, think and act.

There is one other word tucked away in *chayil*. It is the word *train*. Cultivating a strength of mind that enables one to encounter danger without fear, but with firmness, bravery, and courage requires training.

Barak did not just become a leader of an army. Deborah did not just become a judge. God gifted them with the abilities to pursue those callings. But both had to train to become who they were and operate in the submission required of the position they held.

Barak, most likely, started as a foot solider, proved himself capable, and rose to the position of leadership. Deborah had to pray, study the Torah, submit to others for various seasons, learn through experience, and grow in knowledge and understanding. She had to learn how to operate in discernment and wisdom. She did not appoint herself judge. She proved herself, then at the appointed time, stepped into her God-given position.

We tend to idealize other people's lives. Yes, Deborah held a position of honor. But, understand this, she listened to people's problems ALL DAY LONG. So, before you wish away what God has for you because you think you would like to be just like Deborah, count the costs. Embrace and pursue what God has for you, for you are tailored made for it…focus on it and train for it.

Training does not stop. Training is ongoing and it is a constant choice to keep moving forward. Not necessarily in position, but in cultivating a character people are drawn to and what you do, is done with excellence. Position might not change, but sphere of influence will.

A virtuous woman is a woman who is **voluntarily obedient** to Truth. She has an awareness and commitment to do the right thing (by God's Word) regardless of the circumstance or the potential of an adverse reaction by others.

Remember, Abigail went back to her husband, Nabal, and told him what she had done. She knew telling him had the potential to ignite him to wrath. But it was more important to be in right relationship with God. Abigail showed respect to her husband by telling him, regardless of his reaction, what she had done. Please do not apply her actions as a blanket response to every situation, discernment and wisdom are to be pursued for each circumstance.

There is a price to pay when you choose to do the right thing. You might not become the most popular person when you do the right thing. Remember, there is a higher price to pay when you choose things outside of God's Word and Will.

Voluntary obedience is an intentional, intelligent, eyes wide open decision to continually position oneself in God's Will by living according to His commands. This requires trust, which is built and deepened through constant communion with Him and being a student of His Word.

There are incredible examples of virtuous women in the Bible, starting with Eve. She disobeyed God. Her oldest son, Cain, killed her other son, Abel. I cannot imagine having to work through the anger, grief, hatred, love, and every other emotion she had to wrestle through. This statement reveals the strength of mind and the personal bravery she possessed in the midst of the reality of her situation.

> *"she bore a son and named him Seth, 'For God has appointed another seed for me instead of Abel, whom Cain killed.'"* (Genesis 4:25)

She, as so many other imperfect but virtuous women of the Bible, wrestled through her emotions, thoughts, and fears until she resolved herself to trust God above all else…no matter the circumstance.

Chayil comes from *chuwl*, or *chiyl*, pronounced *kheel*. *Chiyl*, a prim root *to twist or whirl* (in a circular or spiral manner), to *dance* or *writhe* in pain (especially of parturition) or fear; to *wait*, to *pervert*; bear, (make to) bring forth, (make to) calve, dance, drive away, fall grievously with pain, fear, form, great, grieve, (be) grievous, hope, look, make, be in pain, be much (sore) pained, rest, shake, sharpen (be) sorrow(-ful), stay, tarry, travail (with pain), tremble, trust, wait carefully (patiently), be wounded (Strong 2342).

Have you ever wanted something so bad that it hurt? Have you ever been in such turmoil over someone else's pain that you would do almost anything to take that pain away from them? It is through this perspective that you need to gain understanding of the type of pain *chiyl* is conveying.

Sarah and Hannah are two women who faced similar situations. Both women were unable to have children.

God told Abram, who became Abraham, and Sarai, who became Sarah, that they would have a child, even though Sarah was past childbearing years. Sarah, rather than waiting on the Lord, took matters into her own hands and had her maidservant, Hagar, go to Abram. Hagar bore a son, Ishmael. Later, Sarah did birth a son, Isaac…the one the Lord told Abraham and Sarah they would have (Genesis 12-22). The consequences of Sarah and Abraham's actions are still with us today. The descendants of Ishmael and Isaac still war against each other.

Hannah was one of two wives of Elkanah. Peninnah, Elkanah's other wife, had children. Hannah did not. Peninnah provoked, ridiculed, and made Hannah miserable…year after year. Hannah, year after year, would go up to the house of the Lord, wept, fasted, and prayed.

> *"And she was in **bitterness of soul**, and prayed to the Lord and **wept in anguish**. Then **she made a vow** and said, "O Lord of hosts, if You will indeed look on the affliction of Your maidservant and remember me, and not forget Your maidservant, but will give Your maidservant a male child, then I will give him to the Lord all the days of his life, and no razor shall come upon his head." (1 Samuel 1:10-11, emphasis added)*

Hannah was praying in such a manner that Eli, the priest, thought she was drunk.

> *And it happened, as she continued praying before the Lord, that Eli watched her mouth. Now **Hannah spoke in her heart**; only her lips moved, but her voice was not heard. Therefore Eli thought she was drunk. So Eli said to her, "How long will you be drunk? Put your wine away from you!"*
>
> *But Hannah answered and said, "No, my lord, I am **a woman of sorrowful spirit**. I have drunk neither wine nor intoxicating drink, but **have poured out my soul before the Lord**. Do not consider your maidservant a wicked woman, for **out of the abundance of my complaint and grief** I have spoken until now."*
>
> *Then Eli answered and said, "Go in peace, and the God of Israel grant your petition which you have asked of Him."*
>
> *And she said, "Let your maidservant find favor in your sight." So the woman went her way and ate, and **her face was no longer sad**. (1 Samuel 1:12-18, emphasis added)*

Hannah is a powerful example of what it means to *chiyl*, to twist or whirl oneself in great pain, travailing in worship, patiently waiting before the Lord to bring forth the hope.

Hannah was mercilessly ridiculed. She was thought to be a drunkard. She suffered mental and emotional abuse for years. But, through faithfulness, she twisted herself into God until she was woven into the beauty of His goodness. Hannah refused to let go of God until He answered her prayers.

Samuel was born to Hannah and Elkanah. True to her vow, once Samuel was weaned, Hannah took him to the Lord. They worshipped the Lord together, and Hannah left her son in service to the Lord. Hannah bore three more sons and two daughters.

And Samuel, he *"grew in stature, and in favor both with the Lord and men."* (1 Samuel 2:26)

God's Will was accomplished in each woman's life. But, because of how each of them chose to bring forth His Will, they had very different consequences associated with them.

Sarah took matters into her own hands and it caused her, her household, and descendants turmoil, strife, and chaos. Hannah chose to *chiyl*, to bring forth through prayer and worship the promises of God. It brought forth blessing to her, her household, and a nation.

Women, such as Rachel, Esther, Dorcas, Elizabeth, Martha, Mary (mother of Jesus), and Anna — to name a few — all faced challenging situations. Yet, they chose to be women of *chayil* who pressed their lives in *chiyl* to overcome great adversity, walk through very difficult situations, and fulfill the commands of God.

Recall Mary at the tomb in the garden. She was weeping, *chiyl*, and Jesus revealed Himself to her.

Their choice to be obedient regardless of the cost, to be brave in the face of adversity, to trust God with the outcome, impacted, and in some instances saved, countless lives.

Behold, imperfect, but strong, brave, intelligent, resourceful, graceful, kind, faithful, virtuous Women. These same types of women surround us every day, and you are counted among them.

> *"Do not let your adornment be **merely** outward — arranging the hair, wearing gold, or putting on fine apparel — rather **let it be the hidden person of the heart**, with the*

incorruptible beauty of a gentle and quiet spirit*, which is **very precious in the sight of God**.*" (1 Peter 3:3-4, emphasis added)

There is nothing wrong with outer bling and taking care of the body. Woman's manner of appearance and dress should reflect the respect she has for God and for herself. But bling, plastic surgery, botox, and revealing shirts and shorts will never genuinely cultivate a healthy self-worth or sincerely validate one's identity.

A virtuous Woman is a woman of quiet strength, confident ability, strategic efficiency, with stored up wealth (resources, in various forms) who brings things forth with the force of an army through discernment, wisdom, and worship.

The heart is at the center of being a virtuous Woman. A heart that is whole, not broken by the trials and disappointments of life, is the anchor to cultivating a noble character. And only God can make and keep our hearts whole. A virtuous Woman puts God and her relationship with Him above all else. She trusts in Him and does not lean on her own understanding. She acknowledges Him in all that she does and knows that He directs her steps.

She is a blessing to others and provides security to those in her care. She is not afraid of work and takes responsibility for herself, her household and sees to the needs of others. She has knowledge and understanding about the commands of God, about the world, and business. She knows her strengths and has wisdom on how to utilize them for the best. She humbly, yet confidently, comprehends the value of her efforts. She is secure in her identity; therefore, she willingly shares her wisdom and knowledge with others so that they can pursue fulfilling their potential. She has no reason to brag for her work speaks for itself.

God deposited within you all the components to become a Virtuous Woman. It is not easy to draw them out, strengthen them, live in them consistently, and endure the challenges that come against you when you're faced with the choice to stand in integrity or compromise.

But you wondrous Woman, it is worth the pursuit. You were destined to be a Virtuous Woman.

Pursue the Beauty of YOU!

Chapter 10

Reflection

1. Why do you think that often time more importance is placed on someone's outward success rather than the integrity of their character?
_____
_____
_____
_____
_____

2. Do you believe people spend more time pursuing outward success rather than inward integrity?
_____
_____
_____
_____

Why or why not?
_____
_____
_____
_____
_____

3. To what degree do you think someone's character embodies the fulfillment of their life?
_____
_____
_____
_____
_____

4. Do you think it is important to cultivate a virtuous character?

Why or why not?

Read the Book of Ruth.

5. What are your general observations about the Book of Ruth?

6. Boaz said that the people of his town knew that Ruth was, *"a virtuous woman."* What thoughts do you have about this statement?

7. Ruth, a foreigner and a widow, is listed in Jesus Christ's genealogy. What does this reveal about the character of God?

It is important to know why you want to become a virtuous woman.

8. Why do you need to have an idea of your "why" in pursing becoming a virtuous woman?
_____
_____
_____
_____
_____

9. Why is it important to know what a virtuous Woman is by God's standard?
_____
_____
_____
_____
_____

10. Why is it necessary to follow God's instructions in becoming a woman of virtue instead of the instructions of others, including your own thoughts on how?
_____
_____
_____
_____
_____

Virtuous, Hebrew: *chayil*, a force, whether of men, means or other resources; an *army, wealth, virtue, valor, strength:* –able, activity (+) army, band of men (soldiers), company, (great) forces, goods, host, might, power, riches, strength, strong, substance, train, (+) valiant (-ly), valour, virtuous (ly), war, worthy (ily) (Strong's 2428 from 2342).

11. Write down your thoughts on Virtuous, *chayil*.
_____
_____
_____
_____
_____

Chayil, denotes a force to be reckoned with, a force coming to help, to bring whatever resources are needed.

12. What does this say about what is within you when you face difficult situations internally or externally?

13a. Are resources limited to one thing?

13b. Why is this important to understand?

Read Judges 4-5.

14. Write down your thoughts on these chapters.

15. Write down a few thoughts about Deborah, Barak and Jael.

_____
_____
_____
_____
_____
_____

16. What does it say about Barak that he was unwilling to go to battle without Deborah?

_____
_____
_____
_____
_____
_____
_____
_____

17. What do you think the outcome would have been if Deborah and Barak put personal interest above the higher threat the enemy presented?

_____
_____
_____
_____
_____
_____

18. What does it reveal about Deborah and Barak's character that they went to battle together?

_____
_____
_____
_____
_____
_____

Virtuous encompasses valor, which is defined as, *strength of mind in regard to danger, that quality which enables one to encounter danger with firmness; personal bravery; courage; intrepidity; and prowess.*

19. What does this definition of Virtuous say to you personally?

_____
_____
_____
_____
_____

Take an inventory of your life in relation to this definition of Virtuous.

20. In what areas of your life are virtuous traits evident?

_____
_____
_____
_____
_____

21. In what areas of your life does virtue need development?

_____
_____
_____
_____
_____

22. What challenges, insecurities, fears do you have that hinder having strength of mind to encounter danger with firmness?

_____
_____
_____
_____
_____
_____

The attributes that define a virtuous Woman do not just happen. Once they are known, they must be developed until they become a part of your nature. They become how you feel, think, and act. Developing a virtuous mindset and character takes work.

23. Why does developing virtue in one's life take training and work?

___

24. How is developing virtue in one's mindset and character an ongoing process?

___

25. Does training ever stop?

___

Why or why not?

___

A virtuous woman is a woman who is ***voluntarily obedient*** to Truth. She has an awareness and commitment to do the right thing (by God's Word) regardless of the circumstance, or the potential of an adverse reaction by others.

26a. In what areas of your life is voluntary obedience to Truth easy for you?

___

26b. Why?

27a. In what areas of your life is voluntary obedience to Truth more difficult?

27b. Why do you think that is?

27c. What steps can you take to become more obedient in these areas of difficulty?

Voluntary obedience is an intentional, intelligent, eyes-wide-open decision to continually position oneself in God's Will by living according to His commands.

28a. What are your thoughts regarding a price we pay for doing the right thing?

28b. What can strengthen you to make the price worth it?

_____
_____
_____
_____
_____

29. What are your thoughts regarding a price paid for doing something outside God's Will?

_____
_____
_____
_____
_____

Chayil comes from *chuwl*, or *chiyl*, pronounced *kheel Chiyl*, a prim root *to twist or whirl* (in a circular or spiral manner), to *dance* or *writhe* in pain (especially of parturition) or fear; to *wait*, to *pervert*; bear, (make to) bring forth, (make to) calve, dance, drive away, fall grievously with pain, fear, form, great, grieve, (be) grievous, hope, look, make, be in pain, be much (sore) pained, rest, shake, sharpen (be) sorrow(-ful), stay, tarry, travail (with pain), tremble, trust, wait carefully (patiently), be wounded (Strong's 2342).

30. What revelation does the meaning of *chiyl* give you?

_____
_____
_____
_____
_____

31. How is the pain in *chiyl* differ from other types of pain we experience?

_____
_____
_____
_____
_____

32. How does understanding the process of *chiyl* equip and empower you to bring forth God's promises in your life?

Review the responses of Sarah and Hannah again. (Genesis 12-22, 1 Samuel 1-2)

33. What price did Sarah pay for taking matters into her own hands rather than waiting on God to bring forth His promise?

34. What did Hannah have to endure while waiting on God?

35. How did Hannah position herself to receive God's blessing?

36. How did Hannah honor God for His answer to her prayers?

_____
_____
_____
_____
_____
_____
_____

37. How did God honor Hannah for keeping her vow to Him?

_____
_____
_____
_____
_____
_____
_____
_____
_____

Women, such as Rachel, Esther, Dorcas, Elizabeth, Mary Magdalene, Martha, Mary (mother of Jesus), and Anna — to name a few — all faced challenging situations. Yet, they chose to be women of *chayil* who pressed their lives in *chiyl* to overcome great adversity, walk through very difficult situations, and fulfill the commands of God.

Take a moment and think about the reality of these women's lives. They did not have superpowers. They were ordinary women facing very difficult, humiliating, even life-threatening situations. It was the individual, personal choice to entrust their lives to God that strengthened them and gave them the boldness to rise to the occasion and overcome adversity.

> *"Do not let your adornment be **merely** outward—arranging the hair, wearing gold, or putting on fine apparel — rather **let it be the hidden person of the heart**, with the **incorruptible beauty of a gentle and quiet spirit**, which is **very precious in the sight of God**."* (1 Peter 3:3-4, emphasis added)

Their actions may have been outward, but it was the hidden resolve of their heart that made them virtuous women.

38. Why is it so important to determine in your heart the type of person you want to be?

39. Why do you think Peter refers to the beauty of a gentle and quiet spirit as incorruptible?

40. Why do you think the incorruptible beauty of a gentle and quiet spirit is very precious in the sight of God?

41. How important is it to you to cultivate the incorruptible beauty of a gentle and quiet spirit within you?

42. What do you think are the benefits of doing so?

A virtuous woman twists and whirls to trust God above all else. She travails to be voluntarily obedient to His leading and commands. She humbly, intelligently, and confidently embraces her identity, gifts, and abilities and uses them to care for herself and come to the aid of others.

43. What are the benefits of becoming a virtuous woman?

44. Is there anything stopping you from pursuing becoming a virtuous woman?

Other Revelations:

Chapter 11

An Overcoming Lifestyle

Life is challenging. We encounter hardships that leave their mark on how we view ourselves, others, and the world. The actions of others may wound our hearts causing us to put up walls in an attempt of self-preservation, but all it brings is loneliness and depression. Many of our own choices have opened the door to shame, disappointment, and pain. Then, even when we are doing all the "right" things, other people's choices can impact our lives in hurtful and difficult ways.

The routine of life can also be a challenge. Every day doing the same thing, waking up, getting ready, going to work (in the house or out of the house), doing the same tasks, dealing with issues, having dinner, going to bed, then repeat. It can become monotonous. Monotonous can become unfulfilling causing one to question oneself, one's value, and one's purpose.

The world, movies, "reality" shows, social media, and the news give us five-minute windows into other people's lives, and our mind starts to think, if only I had their life. Thoughts whisper in our minds similar to: they have it so good, look how cool their life is, my life would be so much better if I had what they had, all my problems would go away if only I had their opportunities, sure, they have it easy because they have money, etc.

This small window into other people's lives is a distorted and unreal perspective into the reality, the truth, of life that can rob us of our joy, peace, and purpose.

An overcoming lifestyle is a way of life that confronts challenges with personal bravery, walks through disappointments with grace, and embraces the routines of life in a healthy and realistic manner that is anchored in Truth. Once again, not yours, mine, or other people's opinions, but the Truth of who God is and His Word. It is also not at the expense of someone else's value, identity, or purpose. In God's Kingdom, someone does not have to become less than so another person can become more than.

God has laid everything before you. It is your choice to follow or not. God will not yield who He is for you to become someone you were not meant to be. He will, however, allow you to choose your own path, and with a broken heart, bear witness to the consequences your choice will bring forth.

God made a way for us to live as He designed life to be lived. And His hope for you is evident in all He has placed within you and before you. He has given you and all humanity the freewill to determine the direction of their life.

Determine, to fix on; to settle or establish, to give a direction to; to influence the choice; that is, to limit to a particular purpose or direction; To resolve; to conclude; to come to a decision.

You must determine what foundation you set your life on and what you base your decisions on. This gives direction and clarity to your life. God has equipped you with the ability to hear intelligently and make choices to govern your life. It is you and you alone who are ultimately responsible and held accountable for how you live.

Isaiah 50:7 was an anchor for me when I was learning how to reconcile with my past mistakes, live in the present, and position my future to abide in the promises of God.

> *"For the Lord God **will help** me; therefore shall I **not be confounded**: therefore have I **set my face like a flint**, and **I know that I shall not be ashamed**."* (Isaiah 50:7, KJV, emphasis added)

*"For the Lord God **will help** me;"*

Help, this one should sound familiar. *Azar*, to surround, protect or aid—help, succour (Strong's 5826).

God WILL help me, so I am not alone in my journey. Succour (succor) gives me great encouragement, literally, to run to, or run to support; hence, to help or relieve when in difficulty, want or distress.

God RUNS TO ME to help when I am in difficulty, want or distress.

*"therefore shall I **not be confounded**:"*

Confounded, *kâlam*, pronounced, *kaw-lawm*, to wound, to taunt or insult:—be (make) ashamed, blush, be confounded, be put into confusion, hurt, reproach, (do, put to) shame (Strong's 3637).

I will not be made to be ashamed, put into confusion, or thrown into disorder. So, anytime I experienced shame, confusion, or disorder, I knew my mindset was getting out of alignment with God's Word.

Confound, to mingle and blend different things, so that their forms or natures cannot be distinguished; to mix in a mass or crowd, so that individuals cannot be distinguished.

Mixing and mingling belief systems, trains of thought, causes dilution and distortion. Therefore, it creates instability and confusion. Neither of those are of God. You must choose your path and be consistent in walking it out.

"I set my face like a flint,"

I made a deliberate determination that I would follow Christ and trust in the promises of God no matter what. I set my face like a flint, hard, and pursued Him. Through every stumble, forgetfulness, old habits rearing their ugly heads, two steps forward, three steps back, I would fall to my knees, ask forgiveness, and get back up again.

I knew what the outcomes were of not following Him and trusting in His Word. I never wanted to go back to those. So, I kept pressing forward, and now, I wish I could say I had it all together. I do not, but I do have peace, joy, fulfillment, purpose, clarity, and so many other blessings. There is no other direction for me but Jesus Christ.

God is faithful and His Word is eternal. I do not look elsewhere to govern my actions or reactions.

"I know that I shall not be ashamed."

Ashamed, bûwsh, pronounced *boosh*; a prim. root; to pale, to be ashamed; to be disappointed, or delayed:—(be, make, bring to, cause, put to, with) shame, be confounded, become dry, delay, be long (Strong's 954).

My face will never turn pale when I trust in the Lord. No one can make me, bring me to, cause me to feel, or put me to shame. I refuse to give people that much power over my identity or worth. God defines me.

God will never disappoint me or be delayed in His help.

Look at this depth of ashamed, *become dry*. Life can dwindle all the life out of you. Difficulties, challenges, abuse, routine can all dry up creativity, passion, joy, even the ability to see all the good things in life.

God blessed humanity to be fruitful and multiply from the very beginning and that requires the refreshing of water.

> *"But his delight is in the law of the Lord, and in His law he meditates day and night.*
>
> *He shall be like a tree planted by the rivers of water, that brings forth its fruit in its season, whose leaf also shall not wither; and whatever he does shall prosper."*
> (Psalm 1:2-3)

I know that I will not become dry, no matter the season, as long as I am planted in the Lord.

Setting the right priorities in your life equips, trains, and transforms you to live an overcoming life. Consistently choosing the right priorities brings order and stability to your life. This allows your mind to be renewed to a new way of thinking, of beholding. Then, your nature begins to be transformed so you respond to everything in a healthy, peace-filled manner, including unexpected or hurtful life events.

Determine your relationship with Almighty God comes first.

Hopefully, we have established this necessity throughout the previous chapters. Everything begins and ends with God. Without Him, everything crumbles.

Determine to live your life as Jesus Christ lived His.

No, you are not Jesus Christ. You are not the Savior, which means you cannot save yourself or others. Only God, through Christ Jesus, can.

But you can model your life after Christ and through your actions and God's Words, you can point people to Jesus Christ, so they too can experience the freedom found in Christ.

Christ lived His life by following The Ten Commandments, the ones He summed up in the New Testament into two commands.

New Testament – Love God.

"Jesus answered him, "The first of all the commandments is: 'Hear, O Israel, the Lord our God, the Lord is one. And you shall love the Lord your God with all your heart, with all your soul, with all your mind, and with all your strength. This is the first commandment." (Mark 12:29-30)

Old Testament – Love God.

"I am the Lord your God, who brought you out of the land of Egypt, out of the house of bondage."

"You shall have no other gods before Me."

"You shall not make for yourself a carved image—any likeness of anything that is in heaven above, or that is in the earth beneath, or that is in the water under the earth; you shall not bow down to them nor serve them. For I, the Lord your God, am a jealous God, visiting the iniquity of the fathers upon the children to the third and fourth generations of those who hate Me, but showing mercy to thousands, to those who love Me and keep My commandments."

"You shall not take the name of the Lord your God in vain, for the Lord will not hold him guiltless who takes His name in vain."

"Remember the Sabbath day, to keep it holy." (Exodus 20:2-8)

New Testament – Love People.

"And the second, like it, is this: 'You shall love your neighbor as yourself.' There is no other commandment greater than these." (Mark 12:31)

Old Testament – Love People.

"Honor your father and your mother, that your days may be long upon the land which the Lord your God is giving you."

"You shall not murder."

"You shall not commit adultery."

"You shall not steal."

"You shall not bear false witness against your neighbor."

"You shall not covet your neighbor's house; you shall not covet your neighbor's wife, nor his male servant, nor his female servant, nor his ox, nor his donkey, nor anything that is your neighbor's." (Exodus 20:12-17)

This is how we model our lives after Jesus. Adhering to God's standard renews our minds and transforms our hearts.

The other element we are to model our lives after Jesus Christ is purpose. The motivation Jesus Christ had to fulfill His purpose was to, *"do those things that please Him"* (John 8:29). Jesus was sent by the Father for a specific purpose, one that only He could fulfill in its fullness, *"the Son of Man has come to seek and to save that which was lost."* (Luke 19:10)

Our motivation should be the same, *"do things that please Him (the Father)."* Our purpose is the same as well, *"to seek and to save that which was lost."* Ours just looks different because, again, we are not the ones who can save. But also, because of how God orchestrated how those who believe in Christ Jesus are to work together.

> *"but, speaking the truth in love, may grow up in all things into Him who is the head — Christ — from whom the whole body,* **joined and knit together by what every joint supplies***, according to the* **effective working by which every part does its share***, causes growth of the body for the edifying of itself in love."* (Ephesians 4:15-16, emphasis added)

Each of us supplies, through our giftings, calling, talents, and work, our piece of what is necessary for the whole body to work together. I encourage you to read 1 Corinthians 12 to gain further understanding of how God knits the body of Christ together. He is genius.

But we become disjointed when we do not first learn how to live an overcoming lifestyle. So, we must continually allow the Word of God to renew and transform us.

Determine to be a Hearer and a Doer of the Word of God.

> *"But be doers of the word, and not hearers only, deceiving yourselves. For if anyone is a hearer of the word and not a doer, he is like a man observing his natural face in a mirror; for he observes himself, goes away, and immediately forgets what kind of man he was. But* **he who looks into the perfect law of liberty and continues in it, and is not a forgetful hearer but a doer of the work, this one will be blessed in what he does.***"* (James 1:22-25, emphasis added)

Do not be deceived. You must determine to apply the Word of God to your life. You must determine to live it out. If you do not, you will forget who you are. If you do, you will be blessed in what you do. The Word of God will transform you knowingly and unknowingly. It is powerful and it will accomplish all that God intends to accomplish in you and through you.

Read, study, and meditate on the Word of God and then put it into practice. It is difficult at first. You are training your mind and muscles to new ways. But, just like consistent exercise, it becomes easier because it brings out who God designed us to be since the beginning.

Determine to be a Holy Spirit-led follower of Jesus Christ.

The Holy Spirit is a gift from God. He is not weird; people have made Him weird out of ignorance or self-glorification. The Holy Spirit is our Helper, Teacher, and Comforter. He has several responsibilities, including guiding us into all Truth, telling us of things to come, and revealing to us those things God has given us.

> *"Now we have received, not the spirit of the world, but the Spirit who is from God, that we might know the things that have been freely given to us by God."* (1 Corinthians 2:12)

The Holy Spirit also gives you power to go about doing good and fulfilling the call of God upon your life. He also empowers you to make the necessary changes in your life to bring forth the fruit of His Spirit.

> *"But the fruit of the Spirit is love, joy, peace, longsuffering, kindness, goodness, faithfulness, gentleness, self-control. Against such there is no law."* (Galatians 5:22-23)

This fruit in your life is a true treasure of living an overcoming life. You know the beauty of kindness if you have ever been abused. You behold the wonder of faithfulness if you have experienced being let down. You are in awe of peace when chaos has ruled your life. The fruit of the Spirit becomes more and more evident in your life as you overcome what you need to overcome.

We all have different things to overcome. It all depends on the life experiences we have had and how they impacted our life. The journey may be different, but the end result is the same, to have the mind of Christ.

2 Corinthians 10:4-5 are two verses that anchored me while I worked with the Lord through my messes. They still anchor me as Mankind and the world keep trying to pervert and distort thinking. The world continues to try to distort God's Word. This is why I need to read, study, and practice the presence of God in the cool of the evenings, so I will be prepared for the midst of the fire.

> *"For the weapons of our warfare are not carnal but mighty in God for pulling down strongholds, casting down arguments and every high thing that exalts itself against the knowledge of God, bringing every thought into captivity to the obedience of Christ,"* (2 Corinthians 10:4-5)

"For the weapons of our warfare are not carnal"

We are natural and spiritual beings. We are also in a natural and spiritual war. There is still a very real enemy whispering in our ears to get us off course, to steal anything he can from us, and kill us mentally, emotionally, spiritually, and even physically. Natural weapons are not effective in the battle the enemy engages in. We cannot fight him in the natural, only in the spiritual armed with the weapons God has provided to us.

Jesus Christ defeated the enemy at the Cross. He disarmed the principalities and powers that held Mankind in bondage. He overcame the powers of darkness, and that victory allows us to fight and also overcome from a place of victorious position.

Those weapons include, but are not limited to, Him, Jesus Christ and the power and authority we have in Him. We have the Holy Spirit, the Word of God, prayer, and our determination to operate our lives within the commands of God.

"but mighty in God for pulling down strongholds,"

The word for strongholds here is *ochyromaton*, and it is only used once. It refers to a fortress. It is something that has been built that is holding one captive. A remote derivative of *ochyromaton* is echo.

The weapons God has given us to engage in battle are to tear down strongholds the enemy has planted through a whisper. Or has used a person who is wounded, broken, insecure, filled with anger, and/or in fear to speak these things to us.

> *"You will never amount to anything."*
> *"You will never change."*
> *"Once an addict, always an addict."*
> *"Failure."*

These can become *"echos"* in our minds, reverberating through our thoughts, reinforcing the belief in them. Only God's Truth can confront and tear down these lies.

An overcoming lifestyle takes every one of those external and internal strongholds and confronts them with the Word of God. Then, you begin to live them out, be a doer, and they will become a part of who you are.

> "You will never amount to anything." Confront it with: *"For I know the thoughts that I think toward you, says the Lord, thoughts of peace and not of evil, to give you a future and a hope."* (Jeremiah 29:11) Then live it out.

> "You will never change." Confront it with: *"But we all, with unveiled face, beholding as in a mirror the glory of the Lord, are being transformed into the same image from glory to glory, just as by the Spirit of the Lord."* (2 Corinthians 3:18) Then live it out.

> "Once an addict, always an addict." Confront it with: *"Therefore if the Son makes you free, you shall be free indeed."* (John 8:36) Then live it out.

> "Failure." Confront it with: *"Not that I have already attained, or am already perfected; but I press on, that I may lay hold of that for which Christ Jesus has also laid hold of me. Brethren, I do not count myself to have apprehended; but one thing I do, forgetting those things which are behind and reaching forward to those things which are ahead, I press toward the goal for the prize of the upward call of God in Christ Jesus."* (Philippians 3:13-14) Then live it out.

Every stronghold, every echo, that holds you or others in bondage and beneath our God-given identity and potential can be pulled down by God's mighty weapon — His Word and His power and authority that backs it up.

"casting down arguments and every high thing that exalts itself against the knowledge of God,"

Arguments, *logismous*, reasoning, thinking, a conception, device. (Strong's 3053). In other words, some limited understanding or philosophy concocted by man, inspired by the enemy, that tries to outthink or out reason God…who is infinite.

Cancel Culture and Critical Race Theory are the philosophies currently attempting to sweep through humanity. Humanity will feel the destruction of its wake for generations if people do not cast it down. When I first heard of Cancel Culture and Critical Race Theory, the names alone gave me pause. But so many people were talking about it, I wanted to become more knowledgeable before I determined how to respond to it.

It was easy for me to reject and cast down the Cancel Culture and Critical Race Theory argument because it does not align with the Word of God.

Any philosophy that promotes and encourages the destruction of another human being simply because they said something someone disagrees with is not of God. Any philosophy that divides groups based on race, gender, culture, or any other category encourages subjection of one to another is not Biblical. Therefore, I have determined that I will not be a part of it. I will not engage in foolish debates about it. I will, however, stand against it.

You may be asking yourself, there was a lot of destruction of other human beings in the Bible. Yes, there was. And God told the Israelites to destroy cities. I am not making excuses for God nor justifying His instructions.

But, when you start to gain a deeper understanding of God's plan and how He navigates His plan through the choices of humanity, it gives you a different perspective. You begin to see God's mercy in all that He does, even in His judgment.

There will always be destruction because humanity has the freewill to choose it. But those who follow Christ and have determined to overcome those debased mindsets, do not rejoice at the destruction of anyone. They know that God will deal with them as He deems just.

> *"Do not rejoice when your enemy falls, and do not let your heart be glad when he stumbles; Lest the Lord see it, and it displease Him, and He turn away His wrath from him."* (Proverbs 24:17-18)

Cancel Culture is based on offense. People are offended due to wounds, insecurity, and fear. God has healed and heals me of wounds and hurtful things I still encounter. I know my God-given identity and any of my short-comings, I work through them with the Lord. I do not need to tear someone else down in order to build myself up. I do not operate in fear because God is my Source.

And I have determined to live an overcoming lifestyle. I have determined that I will not be offended. I do not give other people that much control over my mind or emotions.

"bringing every thought into captivity to the obedience of Christ,"

You have the power to bring every thought that gets whispered in your ear and mind captive. You have control over your thoughts. It is your responsibility to confront every thought with the Word of God and bring it under submission to Jesus Christ.

You will be transformed by the renewing of your mind as you use the weapons of God to pull down every stronghold and you take every thought captive that attempts to exalt itself above the knowledge of God.

> *"For this is the love of God, that we keep His commandments. And His commandments are not burdensome. For whatever is born of God overcomes the world. And this is the victory that has overcome the world our faith. Who is he who overcomes the world, but he who believes that Jesus is the Son of God?"* (1 John 5:3-5)

You will be set free from any bondage. You will walk in peace, not chaos. You will have clarity, not confusion. You will live in faith, not doubt. You will face the challenges of life with confidence, not insecurity. You will not be overcome by evil, but you will have the determination to overcome evil with good. All things are possible in Christ Jesus.

Set your face like flint and live an overcoming lifestyle.

Chapter 11

Reflection

1. What are some of the challenges you are facing now?
___
___
___
___

2. What, if any, walls have you put up to protect yourself from being hurt or disappointed?
___
___
___
___

3a. What choices of others have impacted your life in a challenging way, even though you were doing all the "right" things?
___
___
___
___

3b. How did you handle those?
___
___
___
___
___
___

Routines are a reality of life. They need to be thought of in a healthy, constructive way, otherwise, resentment, frustration, and coveting can steal the joy and the blessing that routine provides.

4a. How much do you struggle with the routine of life?

_____
_____
_____
_____

4b. What thoughts do you wrestle with regarding the mundane things of life?

_____
_____
_____
_____
_____

4c. How do you process through the information and perspective the media, reality shows, and social media provide?

_____
_____
_____
_____
_____

4d. Do you wrestle with anger, jealousy, resentment, and/or a lack of gratitude for what you do have?

_____
_____
_____
_____

Why or why not?

_____
_____
_____
_____

An overcoming lifestyle is a way of life that confronts challenges with personal bravery, walks through disappointments with grace, and embraces the routines of life in a healthy and realistic manner that is anchored in Truth.

5a. Do you want to cultivate an overcoming lifestyle?
_____
_____
_____
_____
_____

Why or why not?
_____
_____
_____
_____
_____

5b. What may hinder you from nurturing an overcoming lifestyle?
_____
_____
_____
_____
_____

5c. Do you believe that there are areas in your life that you need to overcome?
_____
_____
_____
_____

If yes, write them out here.
_____
_____
_____
_____
_____

Determine, to fix on; to settle or establish, to give a direction to; to influence the choice; that is, to limit to a particular purpose or direction; To resolve; to conclude; to come to a decision.

6a. What degree do you take ownership and responsibility to determine the direction of your life?

_____
_____
_____
_____
_____
_____

6b. What percentage do you think your life is still on yours, another's, or the world's direction?

_____
_____
_____
_____
_____
_____

6c. Are you resolved to establish your life on God's direction?

_____
_____
_____
_____
_____
_____

Why or why not?

_____
_____
_____
_____
_____

> *"For the Lord God **will help** me; therefore shall I **not be confounded**: therefore have **I set my face like a flint**, and **I know that I shall not be ashamed**."* (Isaiah 50:7, KJV, emphasis added)

*"For the Lord God **will help** me;"*

7a. Write down what this statement means to you and how it encourages you to pursue an overcoming lifestyle:

_____
_____
_____
_____
_____
_____
_____

7b. Do you believe it?

_____
_____
_____
_____
_____
_____

Why or why not?

_____
_____
_____
_____
_____
_____
_____
_____

7c. What will it take for you to fully believe it?

_____
_____
_____
_____
_____
_____
_____

*"therefore shall **I not be confounded**:"*

8. Write down what this statement means to you and how it encourages you to pursue an overcoming lifestyle.

_____
_____
_____
_____
_____

"I set my face like a flint,"

9a. Write down why determining your resolve to such a degree is important.

_____
_____
_____
_____
_____

9b. What happens when you do not set your face like a flint?

_____
_____
_____
_____
_____

"I know that I shall not be ashamed."

10a. Write down what this statement means to you and how it encourages you to pursue an overcoming lifestyle:

_____
_____
_____
_____
_____

To know is defined **to perceive with certainty**; to understand clearly, **to have a clear and certain perception of truth**, fact or anything that actually exists.

Remember, there is a difference between feeling ashamed of something you did that was against God's commands and being put to shame. Feeling ashamed of disobedience against God's commands should lead to confession and repentance, then restoration. Being made to feel ashamed of who you are, or a constant shame of something you have done in the past is meant to keep you in bondage. It is not of or from God.

10b. Do you put yourself into the bondage of being ashamed?
___
___
___
___

10c. Do you allow the words or actions of others to make you feel ashamed?
___
___
___
___

10d. Do you know that God will not allow you to be put to shame?
___
___
___
___

Ashamed, *become dry*.

11. Write down what this definition of ashamed is saying to you.
___
___
___
___
___

"But his delight is in the law of the Lord, and in His law he meditates day and night. He shall be like a tree planted by the rivers of water, that brings forth its fruit in its season, whose leaf also shall not wither; and whatever he does shall prosper." (Psalm 1:2-3)

12a. How does this verse relate to not becoming dry?

___

12b. What is required to not become dry according to this verse?

___

Setting the right priorities in your life equips, trains, and transforms you to live an overcoming life.

13a. Have you set priorities in your life?

___

13b. If yes, what are they:

___

13c. If no, why not?

13d. What are the benefits of setting your priorities in the correct order?

13e. What are the consequences if you do not have your priorities in the correct order?

14a. What should be your highest priority?

14b. Why?

14c. Is your relationship with God your highest priority?

14d. How does your life reflect your answer?

15a. Have you determined to live your life as Christ lived His?

Why or why not?

15b. What does it mean to live your life as Christ lived His?

15c. What are some instructions on how to live your life as Christ did?
___
___
___
___
___

15d. What areas of your life require more attention to align with Christ's life?
___
___
___
___
___

16. How does aligning our lives with the commandments of God renew our minds and transform our hearts?
___
___
___
___

17a. What was Jesus Christ's motivation for living the life He lived while on earth?
___
___
___
___

17b. How does this help us with our motivation to live as Jesus lived?
___
___
___
___

18a. What was Jesus Christ's purpose in living as He lived?
___
___
___

18b. How is that applicable to our lives?

18c. How is that applicable to how we respond to other's lives?

18d. How is that applicable to how we respond to the world around us?

> "but, speaking the truth in love, may grow up in all things into Him who is the head — Christ — from whom the whole body, **joined and knit together by what every joint supplies**, according to the **effective working by which every part does its share**, causes growth of the body for the edifying of itself in love." (Ephesians 4:15-16, emphasis added)

19a. Whom are we all to grow up into?

19b. How are we connected to each other in Him?

___

19c. What do we individually bring to the whole?

___

19d. Why is it important that every part does it share?

___

19e. Can people who do not have their priorities in order effectively do their share?

___

Read 1 Corinthians 12.

20a. Write down your thoughts regarding how God orchestrated the Body.

___

20b. How well do you think the Body works together if people do not pursue an overcoming lifestyle?

___

20c. Why do you think that is?

___

> *"But be doers of the word, and not hearers only, deceiving yourselves. For if anyone is a hearer of the word and not a doer, he is like a man observing his natural face in a mirror; for he observes himself, goes away, and immediately forgets what kind of man he was. But **he who looks into the perfect law of liberty and continues in it, and is not a forgetful hearer but a doer of the work, this one will be blessed in what he does.**"*
> (James 1:22-25, emphasis added)

21a. Why is it important to be not only a Hearer, but a Doer of the Word?

___

21b. What are you doing to yourself if you are only a Hearer of the Word and not a Doer?

___

21c. What is the danger in forgetting what kind of person you are?

21d. Whose law of liberty are you to focus on?

21e. What do you think James is saying when he says, *"and continues in it"*?

21f. What do you think James is instructing when he says, *"a doer of the work"*?

21g. What is the work he is referring to?

21h. What are the benefits of being a Doer?

The Holy Spirit is a gift from God.

Additional verses on the Holy Spirit for further study: John 14:25-27; Acts 1:8, 2:33, 4:31; Romans 14:16-18; 1 Corinthians 2:13; 2 Corinthians 13:14; 1 Thessalonians 4:8; 2 Timothy 1:14; Titus 3:5; Hebrews 2:4

22a. Describe your current understanding of the Holy Spirit.

22b. How evident is the Holy Spirit working in your life?

22c. What, if anything, is hindering you from becoming a Holy Spirit led follower of Jesus Christ?

The Holy Spirit is your Teacher, Helper, and Comfort. I encourage you to continue to study the Word of God about Him beyond the verses listed above. Go to BibleGateway.com and enter Holy Spirit, Spirit of God, Spirit in the search box. Read through the verses, make sure they refer to the Holy Spirit, and ask for revelation and understanding.

> *"Now we have received, not the spirit of the world, but the Spirit who is from God, that we might know the things that have been freely given to us by God."* (1 Corinthians 2:12)

23a. Who is the Spirit from?

_____
_____
_____
_____
_____
_____
_____
_____

23b. Why is it important to receive Him according to 1 Corinthians 2:12?

_____
_____
_____
_____
_____
_____
_____

> *"But the fruit of the Spirit is love, joy, peace, longsuffering, kindness, goodness, faithfulness, gentleness, self-control. Against such there is no law."* (Galatians 5:22-23)

24a. Why is the Fruit of the Spirit evidence of an overcoming lifestyle?

_____
_____
_____
_____
_____
_____

24b. What importance do you place on cultivating the Fruit of the Spirit in your life?

___

"For the weapons of our warfare are not carnal but mighty in God for pulling down strongholds, casting down arguments and every high thing that exalts itself against the knowledge of God, bringing every thought into captivity to the obedience of Christ," (2 Corinthians 10:4-5)

"For the weapons of our warfare are not carnal"

25a. Why do you think we need weapons?

___

25b. Why is important to understand they cannot be carnal, of the natural world?

___

25c. What is the greatest weapon we have in the battles we face?

___

"but mighty in God for pulling down strongholds,"

26a. What strongholds, if any, do you have in your life?

_____
_____
_____
_____

26b. What "echos," if any, are hindering you?

_____
_____
_____
_____
_____

26c. What do we need to confront any stronghold or echo with?

_____
_____
_____
_____
_____

26d. How often do we need to confront them?

_____
_____
_____
_____

"casting down arguments and every high thing that exalts itself against the knowledge of God,"

27a. What are arguments and every high thing?

_____
_____
_____
_____

27b. When do we know we are to cast them down?

27c. What is the determining factor to when we cast them down?

27d. How do we cast them down?

27e. Whose weapon and authority do we use to cast them down?

> *"Do not rejoice when your enemy falls, and do not let your heart be glad when he stumbles; Lest the Lord see it, and it displease Him, and He turn away His wrath from him."* (Proverbs 24:17-18)

28a. What is an overcoming lifestyle's response to an enemy falling or stumbling?

28b. Why is this important to keep in mind?

"bringing every thought into captivity to the obedience of Christ,"

29a. Why is it important to bring every thought captive?

29b. What do you think happens to your mind and your sense of well-being when you do not bring every thought captive?

29c. What does it mean to bring every thought captive to the obedience of Christ?

29d. How does bringing every thought captive equip you to live an overcoming life?

30. What would it take for you to commit to living an overcoming lifestyle?

Other Revelations:

Chapter 12

A Heart's Hope

God's desire for humanity is evident in how He created us. He created Male and Female in His image and likeness. He imparted His essence into each, so together, a more complete revelation of Him is revealed. He designed a dwelling place of Bliss where Man and Woman would thrive in their purpose.

God's blessing to be *fruitful*, *multiply*, *fill* the earth, *subdue* it, and have *dominion* over His glorious creation reveals His goodness towards humanity.

His joy was evident as He co-labored with *Ish* to name and position the animals in their identities and purpose. His care was revealed when He created *Ishah* to join *Ish* in the beauty of fellowship to tend and keep His glorious Creation. His gentleness evident as He met with them in the cool of the day to see how they were doing.

His self-control towards *Ish* and *Ishah* was revealed when they chose not to trust Him, but instead they chose to listen to the whisper that sought to destroy them.

God's kindness and mercy manifested through removing *Ish* and *Ishah* from the Garden, so they would not live forever with the burden of carrying the knowledge of evil.

His longsuffering revealed through His unwavering plan of restoration and redemption to return humanity to His original design despite humanity's continual cycle of rejection of Him and His Truths.

His love is evident by the unfathomable price paid by His Son, Jesus Christ.

Behold! The Hope of the Father.

Hope, a desire of some good, accompanied with at least a slight expectation of obtaining it.

His hope is for Men of Valor to rise in the *Aleph, Yod, Shin* identity He breathed into them. God desires for Women of Virtue to arise as *Aleph, Shin, Hey* and embrace life with bold, humble confidence.

His hope is for humanity to embrace their gifts and talents and passionately commit them to works of service, so others are blessed. His hope is for humanity to know the thoughts He thinks towards us, thoughts of peace, to give us a future and a hope.

His hope is to meet with you in the cool of the evening to talk about your day. His hope is to be with you in the midst of the fire to deliver, protect, or encourage you.

There is still ultimately one decision He asks each of us to make. In the Garden, He asked Man and Woman not to eat of the Tree of Knowledge of Good and Evil. Since then, He lays before us the one decision to either trust Him and all that encompasses, or not. He has, *"set before us, the way of life and the way of death."*

Decision, determination (firm resolution), as of a question or doubt, FINAL judgment, or opinion; end of a struggle.

There is only a lifestyle that leads to life or a lifestyle that leads to death. His hope is for you to embrace life.

With firm resolution, proclaim a final judgment and end your struggle of trying to live by two standards. Pursue Him and His righteousness above all else.

Determine to choose and pursue the higher calling always. It is not always easy. God never said it would be, but He did promise to be with you always. And He has given us Jesus Christ through whom nothing is impossible.

From this day forward, give all diligence to being transformed from glory to glory. Every step, decide to behold the beauty in you and all around you.

Marvel at the wonder of God-given masculinity and encourage Men to rise up to be the *Aleph, Yod, Shin* they were created to be. Men do not need to become less than for Women to become who God created them to be. Within every Man awaits the destiny to become a Man of Valor.

Embrace the beauty of God-given femininity and inspire Women to live in the splendor of *Aleph, Shin, Hey*. Women do not need to be in competition with other Women, or even Men, to become who she was created to be. Within every Woman awaits the destiny to become a Woman of Virtue.

Every day give all diligence to becoming all that is within you to be.

Keep building upon what you have been given, complement your faith by becoming a person of wondrous character.

Continually deepen your spiritual understanding by spending time with the Father and in His Word.

Discipline yourself to be alert to things that are happening around you so you can be quick to respond with God's strategy.

Be a Woman of passionate patience so those around you can experience the grace and mercy of God.

Behold with reverence the splendor and wonder of this amazing gift called life. And always remember majesty can still be found as you are passing through the challenging seasons.

Be friendly with genuine warmth to others so others can encounter the goodness of God.

Be generous to love as God has been generous with His love for you.

When you do these things, no day will pass without its reward as you mature in your experience of our Savior Jesus Christ. (2 Peter 1:5-9)

Let nothing stop you from becoming all of God's hope for you!

Behold! The Beauty of Hope.

Chapter 12

A Heart's Hope

Hope, a desire of some good, accompanied with at least a slight expectation of obtaining it.

1. What new revelation or understanding do you have regarding God since the beginning of Behold?

_____
_____
_____
_____
_____
_____
_____
_____

2. What difference has it made in how you view Man?

_____
_____
_____
_____
_____
_____
_____

3. What difference has it made in how you view Woman?

_____
_____
_____
_____
_____
_____
_____

4. What has changed in your understanding how God created Man and Woman to reveal more of Him?

_____
_____
_____
_____
_____

5. Have you embraced that you are blessed by God to be *fruitful, multiply, fill, subdue,* and have *dominion* over environments for God's glory?

_____
_____
_____
_____
_____

6. How was God's joy revealed in His creation of Male and Female?

_____
_____
_____
_____
_____

7. How was God's care revealed in His creation of *Ish* and *Ishah*?

_____
_____
_____
_____
_____

8. How was God's gentleness revealed in His consistent meeting with *Ish* and *Ishah* in the cool of the day?

_____
_____
_____
_____
_____

9. How was God's self-control revealed when He knew *Ish* and *Ishah* chose to trust the voice of another?

10. How are you at listening to God's voice, rather than the voice whispering to go a different path?

11. How was God's kindness and mercy revealed through removing *Ish* and *Ishah* from the Garden?

12. Do you think that God's kindness and mercy also moves you from harmful situations?

13. Do you trust Him to do that for you?

14. How do you see God's hand in the turns of history to bring forth His plan of restoration and redemption?

_____
_____
_____
_____
_____

15. What are new revelations you have about God's love through this journey together?

_____
_____
_____
_____
_____

16. What does it do to your understanding and knowledge of God to know His hope has always been for humanity to be restored to Him?

_____
_____
_____
_____
_____

17. What does it mean to you to know that God wants to meet with you in the *"cool of the day"*?

_____
_____
_____
_____
_____

18. Have you made your decision to follow Him and His ways?

_____
_____
_____
_____
_____

19. Are you firm in your determination to adhere to His commands so that it will go well with you?

_____
_____
_____
_____
_____

20. Have you given final judgment to be renewed and transformed as you live in a completely new lifestyle?

_____
_____
_____
_____
_____

21. What can you do to encourage Men to become Men of Valor?

_____
_____
_____
_____
_____

22. What can you do to encourage Women to become Women of Virtue?

_____
_____
_____
_____
_____

23. Write down your thoughts regarding this breakdown of 2 Peter 1:5-9, THE MESSAGE:

_____
_____
_____
_____
_____

"So don't lose a minute in building on what you've been given,

complementing your basic faith

with good character,

spiritual understanding,

alert discipline,

passionate patience,

reverent wonder,

warm friendliness,

and generous love,

each dimension fitting into and developing the others.

With these qualities active and growing in your lives, no grass will grow under your feet,

no day will pass without its reward

as you mature in your experience of our Master Jesus.

***Without these qualities you can't see what's right before you**, oblivious that your old sinful life has been wiped off the books."* (2 Peter 1:5-9, THE MESSAGE, emphasis added)

24. Spend a quiet moment with the Father. Ask Him what His hope is for you. Write down everything that comes to your mind.

___

The journey is just beginning.

Behold! The Beauty of Woman.

Resources

Freedom Church

FindFreedom.church

Freedom Church in Carrollton, Texas, is my home church. It is where God has planted me to grow in my relationship with Him and to build relationships with a community of Christ followers. Our vision is to help people find freedom through a personal relationship with Jesus Christ. If you live in the North Texas area and are looking for a home church, I hope you will visit. Every follower of Christ should be rooted in a local, Bible teaching, Holy Spirit-led, restoration believing, saint equipping, community serving, church.

Better Marriage 365

BetterMarriage365.com

Kendall and Starla Bridges, the Lead Pastors of Freedom Church, have a marriage ministry. Their story of broken to better is a story of how God can redeem and restore marriages. Healthy and fulfilling marriages require work. They offer multiple options from books, workbooks, speaking at services and conferences to encourage and equip all marriages to be better through the grace and goodness of God. They challenge all couples to "Never Settle for Good Enough."

The Quest Life – The Fellowship of the Sword

TheQuestLife.com

I highly recommend participating in one of The Quest Life – The Fellowship of the Sword events. These incredible men and women who facilitate these events create an environment where participants can encounter the presence of God and be forever changed.

Additional Resources:

We live in an incredible time. There is so much access to resources to acquire knowledge and understanding. Remember, knowledge should never replace your relationship with God. Knowledge should always be processed with the wisdom and revelation that comes from Almighty God on how to apply it.

I use multiple resources and then compare them to the Holy Bible to bring balance, and to make sure personal opinion or denominational doctrine is not skewing the information…including my own. There is a difference between my current level of revelation and understanding verses inserting a personal thought or opinion and attributing it to the Lord or His Word. My revelation and understanding will increase as I pursue the Lord and study His Word.

Strong's Exhaustive Concordance of the Bible
The Strong's Concordance provides you with depths and dimensions of definitions that today's understanding of words does not convey.

There are treasures in the Holy Bible that can only be revealed when you study past the initial and current definition / understanding of the words.

Bible Gateway
BibleGateway.com
I love this online resource. Bible Gateway provides quick and easy access to find individual verses, themes, and stories, all through a key word search. It provides additional study tools, commentaries, reading plans, and so much more, including different versions / translations of the Holy Bible. The Message is written in contemporary language while the King James Version was written in the flow of 1611, when it was released, beautifully done, but can be challenging to read since we do not speak in the same manner.   Remember, Strong's Concordance is based on the King James Version.

Bible Study Tools
BibleStudyTools.com
Bible Tools is another online resource I use when studying the Word of God. It provides additional information, insights, articles, definitions, and topical studies to increase knowledge and broaden understanding of the Holy Bible.

Webster's Dictionary 1828
WebstersDictionary1828.com
In my opinion, the English language has become diluted from the eloquence and richness of its history. I utilize the Webster's Dictionary because it provides definitions with their original meaning. Additionally, many of the words are defined with applicable Scriptures.

Matthew Henry's Commentary

I enjoy reading commentaries on the Holy Bible. They provide perspectives and understanding that might not cross my mind. To me, it is much like having a conversation with someone and they say something that prompts a thought. I have hard copies of Matthew Henry's Commentary, but Bible Gateway provides access to this commentary as well as others.

Chabad

Chabad.org

The Old Testament is a history of the Jewish people. It is important to have some understanding of the people, times, and customs to be able to put the stories into a proper context. I found some helpful information in this resource.

En-Gedi Resource Center

EnGediResourceCenter.com

This resource provides information to better understand the Holy Bible and Jesus Christ by presenting resources to study them in original context. It gives excellent references to the land, people, and cultures to put the stories in the Bible into the proper perspective.

Acknowledgements

Freedom Church, Carrollton, Texas

FindFreedom.church

I realize I am partial, but the people of Freedom Church are amazing. They are absolutely incredible people. Freedom Family, thank you for doing life together. A special shout out to the Prayer Partners, Missions Team, and Discipleship Classes friends who enrich my life beyond words.

Freedom Family, keep pursuing Jesus and fulfilling the vision of the House to help people find freedom *through a personal relationship with Jesus Christ*. It is my prayer that each of you experience the goodness of God in wondrous ways every day. Thank you for allowing me to do life with you!

Kat Caldwell / Pencils and Lipstick

KatCaldwell.com

Kat and I have been friends for a few years. She used her talents and gifts to help me finish Behold. She is an amazing woman, wife, mother, and writer. Her passion for writers and stories is evident in all that she does. If you are interested in building a relationship with fellow writers, storytellers and overall lovers of all type of writing, this is the community for you.

Cynthia Walsworth / Culture Red

Culture-red.com

Ty and Cindy Walsworth are passionate about creativity. Cindy has been instrumental in getting Behold to the finish line. Culture Red is a creative agency based in Dallas, Texas. If you need help launching your dream, Culture Red might be the agency to guide you through the creative and marketing process.

About the Author

Tracy L. Edwards was born and raised in south Texas. She grew up in the country raising show animals and riding horses at rodeos. She married her husband Steve in 1995 and they have three children and two grandchildren. She enjoys reading, writing, attempts gardening, going on adventures with her family, and working with her husband on their land. Her passion is to see people experience the love of God and fulfill the purposes they were born for. Her heart is to see people live in the hope, peace, and joy that is available through the truth found in a personal relationship with Jesus Christ.

She loves to speak, teach, and equip others to embrace a live lived with passion and purpose.

You can contact her at:

Email: up-word@outlook.com

Website: Up-WordBound.com

Other Books by Tracy L. Edwards

      Created to Be Me / *Living in Your Destiny Every Day*
      Made Free / *Embrace a Life Lived in Freedom*

www.ingramcontent.com/pod-product-compliance
Lightning Source LLC
Chambersburg PA
CBHW081153070526
44583CB00021B/2816